Mountain Biking
— in the —
SCOTTISH
HIGHLANDS

Volume 2

AUTHOR'S NOTE

The success of my first book of tours, called simply

Mountain Biking in the Scottish Highlands

has encouraged me to produce another one. I should like to emphasize that the tours described in this, Volume 2, are quite different to those in the first volume.

Mountain Biking
— in the —
SCOTTISH HIGHLANDS
Volume 2

FRANCES FLEMING

Alexander Heriot

Alexander Heriot & Co. Ltd
P.O. Box 1, Northleach
Cheltenham, Gloucestershire GL54 3JB

ISBN 0-906382-11-4

First published 1992
© 1992 text and maps D. F. Fleming

Design and production by Colin Reed
Typeset by Gilcott Graphics, Rushden, Northamptonshire
Printed and bound in Great Britain by
Woolnough Bookbinding Ltd, Irthlingborough, Northamptonshire

Contents

Maps

A general map of Scotland is on page viii
Each route has its own area map and contour profile

To
The Pirate
with thanks for it all

Acknowledgements

As all Oscar winners say, ''I could not have done it alone''. I shall not go so far as to thank my mother and father for having me, but this book would not have been completed without the kind help of various individuals: Alasdair Ross, Alastair Loder, Jan and Willie Orr, Tom and Chris Bowes, Don Sargeant, Arthur Stewart, Craig MacDonald, the patient staff of Dingwall Public Library and, last but not least, JR.

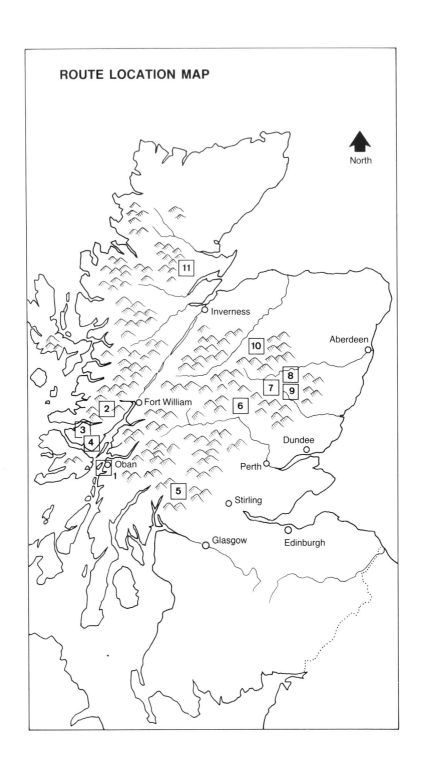

ROUTE LOCATION MAP

North

11

Inverness

10

Aberdeen

8

7 9

Fort William

2

6

3

4

Dundee

Oban

1

Perth

5

Stirling

Glasgow

Edinburgh

Introduction

Scotland in general and the Highlands in particular offer some of the finest mountain biking country imaginable. The hills and glens provide pleasures and challenges in such profusion and of such variety that it is difficult to decide which are the 'best' routes. Some of you may prefer the comparative safety of the tracks at Aviemore, others the more technical and remote trails of Ardnamurchan.

This guide aims to have something for everyone, whether you are a go-it-alone dedicated enthusiast, a holiday group, family or pensioner. There are tours of different length, of different grades of difficulty and of varying ratios of track to tarmac so that everyone of whatever age or ability, from couch potato to Olympic aspirant, will find something to their taste.

Most of this book is self-explanatory but there are some background aspects to bicycling in Scotland, as distinct from other countries, of which overseas visitors may have little or no knowledge and these deserve a mention.

Public Access

There is, in Scotland, no automatic right of access over someone else's land. You must either have the owner's permission to be on his land or you must use a 'public right of way' (see below). And even though the land looks completely desolate and unpopulated it will always have an owner, whether it is a private individual, the Forestry Commission, the National Trust or whoever. There is no specific penalty for trespass, since damage or nuisance must first be proved, but it is within the legal rights of the owner or his representative to remove any trespasser who declines to leave voluntarily.

So much for the theory. In practice, however, there exists in Scotland a long tradition of consideration and co-operation between landowners and walkers and permission is seldom refused for sensible land use so long as it does not interfere with other activities (see Periods of Restricted Access, page 3). If therefore, you intend to leave the public right of way, it is worth making the effort to find someone who can give you the necessary permission. Not only is it an act of courtesy but also one of commonsense since landowners and their employees invariably know useful things like how far the next shop is, who has the best B&B in the area, whether a river is fordable, which footbridge has been swept away in the winter and so on. Moreover, landowners provide, free of charge, much of the bothy accommodation (see page 6) that you may wish to use. So it makes sense and costs nothing to ask permission before camping or leaving the beaten track.

All the tours in this book are on trails and tracks which are public rights of way. These have their roots in history and have developed from the days before the invention of the motor car and the subsequent growth of the present road system. As all journeys were then necessarily made on foot or horseback or by horse-drawn vehicles, traditional cross-country routes became established − old drove roads, military roads, Kirk roads, estate roads − for regular use by the public. Most rights of way are clearly marked on the Ordnance Survey maps. It must also be mentioned that because bicycling involves muscle rather than engine power, so bicyclists have the same legal entitlements on public rights of way as do walkers. But this must not be abused. Walkers very understandably resent bikers who force them off the path or otherwise behave selfishly − and at the moment there are more walkers than bikers!

Part of the attraction of these wild and remote places is the lack of any evidence that another human being was there before you, so if you are intending to camp on any of these tours, please use your commonsense; *do not* light your fire in the middle of a smooth green sward but find somewhere else, i.e. a gravel patch or beach where remains can easily be buried or destroyed. By the same token *do not* leave your sardine tins or empty crisp packets around − take your rubbish with you.

Fire
You may find it hard to believe in a country famous for its rainfall, but fire is one of the greatest hazards in Scotland. The most dangerous time is between March and June when the new season's growth has yet to emerge and the ground is covered in piles of long, dry, dead grass from winter. An ill-considered camp-fire, a burning match, even a casually thrown cigarette-end − any of

these can, in a few moments, start a blaze that will eventually cover hundreds of acres and destroy not only the natural flora but also the nest, eggs or chicks of ground-nesting birds. Trees are especially vulnerable to fire: what little natural woodland remains in Scotland has a tough enough existence already with grazing animals and harsh weather conditions contributing to make its life a fragile one.

A simple rhyme to remember at all times —

That which burns
never returns.

Follow the Code

An easy code to follow is the Off-Road Code issued by the Mountain Bike Club:

- Only ride where you have the legal right
- Always yield to horses and pedestrians
- Avoid animals and crops wherever possible
- Take all litter with you
- Leave all gates as found
- Never create a fire hazard
- Keep unnecessary noise to a minimum
- Always try to be self-sufficient for you and your bike
- Always tell someone where you are going and when you will return.

Periods of Restricted Access

There are times when it is imperative to get permission locally before leaving a public right of way. These are:

- The lambing season (mainly April and May).
- The grouse shooting season (from August 12th through September).
- The deer stalking season (normally August to mid-October).

Remember that you are on holiday but that others have to earn their living from the countryside. If you insist on biking through a flock of sheep that a man has spent the whole day 'gathering' in the surrounding hills, do not be surprised if you get an unfriendly reception when you meet him and his dogs.

3

Best Times

The best months for bicycling in Scotland are May and June — the summer rains have yet to start and the midges are still in hiding. Nevertheless waterproofs should be carried at *all times* (see page 5) and midge repellant should not be eschewed during the midge season — approximately July, August and September.

Many of the tours necessitate fording rivers and burns which can rise and fall very rapidly, a gentle crossing becoming an impassable torrent in a short time — plan accordingly.

Because of the distance between shops, early closing and Sunday observance, it is always advisable to carry some food — and watch your petrol if you are travelling by car.

The Bike

A sturdy well-maintained mountain bike is essential for the tours in this guide — it will be subject to copious amounts of water, mud, rocks and peat, often all at once.

Since all of these tours involve some amount of tarmac riding, you might consider a combination tyre. These have knobs for traction as well as a centre head for quieter performance and lower friction on tarmac, most tyre-manufacturers make such a tyre — consult a bike shop for details. Whichever one you choose, a width of 1.9″ (4.75cm) seems to be a good compromise between rolling well on tarmac yet providing good off-road performance.

A comfortable saddle is a must: few things can make a ride more miserable than saddle sores. While there are many styles of seats available, and choosing the right one for you is vital, it is far more important to spend time on your bike 'hardening' your body to the saddle.

While many say they are confining, toe-clips greatly enhance your performance on the bike and once you have become used to them, you will wonder how you ever rode without them. They are an inexpensive way to upgrade your performance.

Brakes should be checked regularly and kept in close adjustment. If the going is wet and muddy, it helps to clean the grooves in the brake pads regularly.

A working knowledge of the bike and basic emergency repair is imperative. The terrain these tours cover is very conducive to flat tyres, broken spokes, jammed chains, etc., all of which are only a minor inconvenience to someone with tools and know-how but are a distinct disaster to anyone not so equipped. There are many bicycle repair manuals and bike shop professionals available to help you put together a small tool kit and to familiarise you with emergency repairs. Take the time to learn before heading off into the wilds; replacing an inner-tube during a rainstorm on a windswept moor is a far less distressing thought if you have practised it a few times over a pint in front of the fireplace − mind you it's still a pretty distressing thought! In Scotland, bicycle shops with the parts and expertise required by today's hi-tech mountain bikes are few and far between (see page 107), and these tours can be hard on the bikes − be prepared.

Clothing

Due to the variability of Scotland's weather, which can change almost at the blink of an eye, it is wise to be prepared for anything that nature might throw at you, regardless of the forecast or how fine the morning may be.

Several light layers are better than one heavy one as you are better able to control your temperature by adding or removing clothes. The outermost layer should be a waterproof of some kind (preferably a breathable fabric, expensive but worth it), and all layers should allow plenty of movement and be comfortable.

Padded cycling shorts are a must for such long distances: they are extremely comfortable and will save wear and tear on your bum. Likewise a pair of padded cycling gloves will make riding (and falling) more comfortable and will help to prevent the numbness many mountain bikers experience after long hard rides.

While bicycle touring shoes are good, any comfortable pair of trainers or tennis shoes will do as well. It is important that they do not fit too loosely as blisters can result.

I would advise you to wear a helmet − the terrain is difficult, help can be a long time coming and falling off is easy − but of course the choice is yours.

Since many of the directions in the Route Logs necessarily refer to points of the compass, it is highly advisable to include one in your kit. This may seem a needless precaution on a fine and cloudless day but anyone who has been caught in the hills by the sudden descent of an impenetrable layer of mist will know how easy it is to lose one's bearings completely.

Bothies

In several of the remote mountain areas in Scotland, you will come across what appears to be abandoned cottages. These are bothies which are left open for the use of passers-by. They belong to and are made available by the estate on whose land they are situated. Many are in the care of the Mountain Bothies Association, a voluntary working association whose stated object is ''to maintain simple unlocked shelters in remote areas''. You are therefore requested to be careful of their use since misuse can lead to the loss of a valued facility. The quality of bothies is variable and depends on the level of maintenance, popularity and most importantly the habits of those who use them. Those relevant to these tours were pretty immaculate at the time of writing. If you are seriously depending on them as part of your itinerary it would be wise to check with the estate concerned that they are still in use. A list of appropriate telephone numbers is on page 110. Be warned that during the holiday season and weekends some of the more popular ones can become extremely crowded.

About this Guide

I have attempted to begin and end each tour at the same place. Where this was not possible the routes begin and end at railway stations. The only exception to this rule is the Glen Esk – Glen Tanar route which was just too good to be left out. The mileages (km) indicated in the logs are based on cycle computers and will vary in some cases from your own mileages because of such factors as weight difference, tyre pressure and those times you have to shoulder the load.

The maps and profiles provided have been specifically designed to be used in conjunction with the Ordnance Survey (OS) Landranger maps listed at the beginning of each tour and *not* by themselves. Much of Scotland is vast and remote and the weather can change suddenly and dramatically: it would be foolish and dangerous not to consult the appropriate maps regularly.

Scotland is a country as yet largely unspoilt by the hand of man and if it is to remain this way, the mountains and glens, which owing to their very remoteness are mostly tourist-free, must be treated with the greatest respect. Mountain biking in America is causing one of the most divisive storms to blow through the national conservation movement in recent memory. In parks near San

Francisco, Rangers have been forced to close routes, set up speed-traps and use radar guns to curb the fast and reckless riding which is causing erosion and damage to the landscape and driving hikers and equestrians from the trails. Bikers in the US reply that their sport is an efficient, safe, fitness-promoting way to get back to nature and that it rarely interferes with the pleasures of others. Nevertheless their burgeoning numbers have caused safety and ecological concerns and prompted pleas from all over the country to ban them. This may seem a far cry from Scotland but in Britain and the rest of Europe mountain biking is on the increase and we ignore what is happening in America at our peril.

It is ironic that it is our love for the mountains and remote tracks and trails that may also spoil them. Simple actions can make all the difference − never skid or lock your wheels when braking and avoid riding across ground which is easily eroded, i.e. scree, bogs, etc. If our behaviour to the environment and to the people who live and work in it is considerate at all times then we shall be responsible for helping keep intact the romance and integrity of Scotland's remarkable landscape.

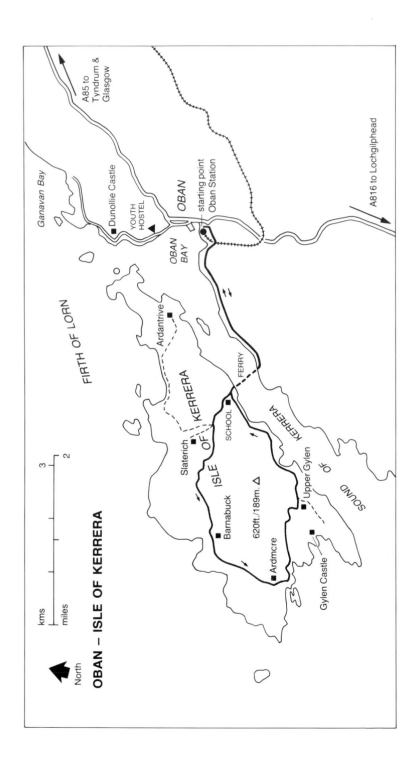

OBAN – ISLE OF KERRERA

North

kms
miles

FIRTH OF LORN

Ganavan Bay

Dunollie Castle
YOUTH HOSTEL

OBAN

starting point
Oban Station

OBAN BAY

A85 to Tyndrum & Glasgow

A816 to Lochgilphead

Ardantrive

ISLE OF KERRERA

Slaterich

SCHOOL

FERRY

Barnabuck

620ft./189m. △

Ardmcre

Upper Gylen

SOUND OF KERRERA

Gylen Castle

1

Oban – Isle of Kerrera

Area information

Oban (Gaelic for Little Bay) is the capital of Lorn, an area which takes its name from Lorn the son of Erc, who ruled it around A.D. 500. Its boundaries are Loch Leven to the north, Loch Craignish to the south and Loch Awe to the west. Today Oban is a centre of West Highland tourism, not only on account of its fine scenery but also because it is the main port for the ferries to the Western Isles.

Standing on the seafront looking up at the town, you can see McCaig's Folly, a round tower sitting somewhat out of place directly above the town centre. It was built by John McCaig, an Oban banker, between 1890 and 1900, with the good intention of aiding unemployed masons. The work was then abandoned when the walls were completed. In 1970 the interior was made into a garden. The best viewpoint in Oban is from the top of Pulpit Hill above the south harbour. At the north end of the town, Corran Esplanade merges into Ganavan Road which leads you past the great rock on which Dunollie Castle is poised over the sea. A few hundred yards before the castle is a tall rock pillar, the Clach a' Choin (Dog Stone), so called because the legendary Fingal used to tie his mighty hunting-dog Bran to it. Fingal was a third-century Irish hero, Fionn MacCoul (called Fingal by the Scots – his name means Chief of Valour in Gaelic), who defended the Hebrides against early Viking pirates. He died in battle in A.D. 283. His son was Ossian who became famous in his own right as a Gaelic bard. The exact date of the construction of Dunollie Castle is not known. Much of the existing castle would have been built by Dughall, the eldest son of Somerled, the Lord of the Isles, who received the Lordship of Lorn in the twelfth century. The clan Dougall are descended from Dughall and this is very much MacDougall country. In 1306 John MacDougall, Lord of Lorn, attacked Robert the Bruce who was then on his way to Loch Awe. Bruce escaped but left the brooch which had bound his cloak in the dying grasp of one of MacDougall's men. The brooch has since become known as the Brooch of Lorn and remains in the hands of John's descendants.

One of the MacDougalls' strongholds is on the island of Kerrera − Gylen Castle. It has a wild site on a rock pillar jutting up from the sea's edge. The name comes from the Gaelic 'Caistal nan Geimhlean', meaning Castle of the Fountains, for its two towers (of which only one is still standing) were built beside natural springs. The castle was built in 1587 but in the covenanting wars of 1647 it was beseiged by a detachment of General Leslie's army at the instigation of the Duke of Argyll (those Campbells again!). The castle was captured and burnt and all the MacDougall defenders were slaughtered. There may have been an earlier fort on the island, for it was invested in July 1249 by Alexander II, who had come to enforce his power over Ewen of Lorn who paid homage to Norway. Alexander spent the night on his ship anchored in Horseshoe Bay where he dreamt that St Columba appeared to him and commanded his return. His men urged him to heed the dream but Alexander refused. As soon as he landed on Kerrera he became ill and died before he could be taken off. The place where he died is called Dalrigh (King's Field).

Kerrera is four miles in length and the highest hill is 620ft (189m). On the west side, by Barnabuck House, is the pier where the crofters and farmers from Mull would land their sheep and cattle, then walk them down to Ardmore from where they would be ferried to the mainland markets. The school was built in 1872 and doubles as a church: previously the islanders would have had to cross to the mainland to worship.

Map: OS Landranger no. 49

Distance: 10.60 miles, 17 kilometres

Difficulty: easy

Time: half a day − it can take longer if your schedule and the ferryman's don't coincide!

Logistics: by train on the Glasgow to Oban line or by car − from the north on the A828, from the east on the A85(T) from the south on the A816(T).

Route description

04.13 miles (06.60km) tarmac, 06.47 miles (10.40km) track/trail.

There are no services once you have left Oban so plan accordingly. Oban has all facilities — mountains of tartan and shortbread, woolly shops, bed and breakfasts, hotels, a youth hostel, etc. The tourist information office is in Argyll Square (see map) and they can give you the times of the ferry across to Kerrera. There is a wealth of cafes and pubs, most of which are fine if you want chips and grease. If you are feeling like a big fluffy omelette filled with crispy bacon, fresh chives and sour cream with tacos on the side, I can recommend a little surfing cafe in Hawaii — but in the meantime try the Lorn in Stevenson Street which usually provides very good soup and seafood, or the Oban Inn on the corner of the main seafront by the north pier — both have good music and occasionally an excellent live band in the evening.

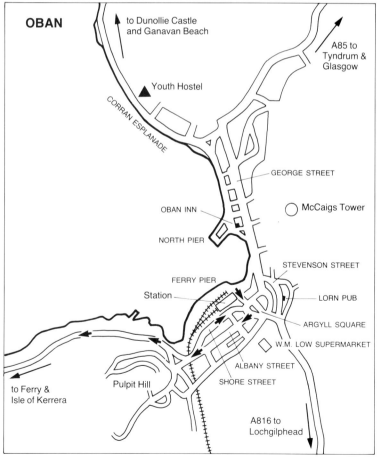

When I rode this tour it was on a mega-hot windless day (yes, they do happen in Scotland!) and if you are in the area with similar conditions then I can recommend nothing finer than this gentle route round Kerrera. The steepest part is right at the beginning and after that it is gently undulating with a couple of good downhills. The track is good quality except for half a mile between Barnabuck and Ardmore. Despite being so close to the mainland, the atmosphere on this island is magic with that timeless quality of the more distant Scottish islands. I was in fact sorely tempted not to return to Oban.

Route Log

00.00m (00.00km) Train station. Head towards Caledonian Hotel and at the junction by the bus stop turn right.

00.04 (00.06) Telephone box. Go round roundabout and take the exit signposted Gallanach and ferry.

00.16 (00.25) Police station and telephone box.

00.28 (00.45) Keep straight − follow ferry sign.

00.38 (00.61) Ferry terminal on the right, keep straight.

00.56 (00.90) Manor House Hotel and restaurant on the right.

02.07 (03.33) Kerrera ferry. At the time of writing £1 each way and 50p per bike.

02.12 (03.41) Telephone box.

02.17 (03.49) Fork, bear right.

02.27 (03.65) School, gate.

02.52 (04.05) Gate and farm.

02.67 (04.29) Gate and fork, bear left.

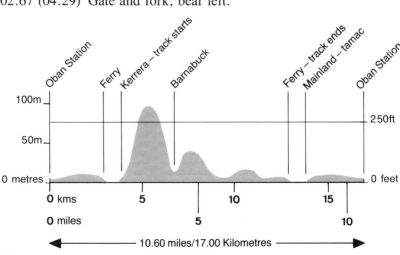

04.27 (06.87) Barnabuck House, lovely camping place. Track becomes grassy.

04.53 (07.28) Track becomes indistinct for a short distance.

04.80 (07.72) Small ford.

05.08 (08.17) Small ford.

05.35 (08.60) Scrappy downhill, running water and stony.

05.41 (08.70) Ardmore Cottage, ruin. Bear right then left. Wonderful views south.

05.50 (08.84) Ford.

05.71 (09.18) Glimpse of Gylen Castle on the right.

06.16 (09.91) Fine view of the castle to the right.

06.22 (10.00) Lower Gylen House.

06.63 (10.66) Upper Gylen House and ruin, bear left.

07.80 (12.55) Fork, keep straight.

08.43 (13.56) Rejoin road to the pier.

08.54 (13.74) Ferry.

10.30 (16.57) Road bears left.

10.54 (16.95) Roundabout, take first left.

10.60 (17.00) Train station.

Looking west down Loch Shiel

2

Glenfinnan – Loch Shiel

Area information

One of the main reasons for the existence of the West Highland Railway was to provide communication with the remote communities of the west coast of Scotland and the Western Isles. The first revenue-earning train left Fort William for Glasgow at 6.10 am on August 7th, 1894. But if the line were to survive, the terminal could not remain at Fort William. The railway had to reach the sea, at Mallaig, where it could pick up the valuable fish traffic. Although Fort William is situated on the shore of a sea loch (Loch Linnhe), it is far from the fishing grounds.

Both the engineers and the contractors employed in the construction of the Mallaig line were from Glasgow. The head of the contractors, Robert MacAlpine, was known as ''Concrete Bob'' because of his enthusiasm for that relatively new building material. For the next five years MacAlpine was to be the central figure in the greatest concentration of concrete construction in the world. The labour force consisted of Irishmen, Lowland Scots, Highlanders, Scandinavians, and Islanders who spoke only Gaelic. The largest camp was established at Lochailort, eventually housing 2,000 of the 3,000 navvies who worked on the line. The old schoolhouse was converted into an eight-bed hospital, the first such building ever to be set up at a construction site in Britain.

At the start the contractors were confident that they would have the line ready for the summer of 1890 but unforeseen difficulties slowed them up – four extra tunnels were needed and MacAlpine had great difficulty in retaining good men because (surprise, surprise) the weather was unusually wet and disagreeable.

The bridges along the line were built of concrete, most of them in standard spans of 50ft. The most spectacular viaduct is that at Glenfinnan which uses twenty-one standard spans.

Thanks to some innovative building techniques and concrete, the battle to build the Mallaig line through glens, under mountains and

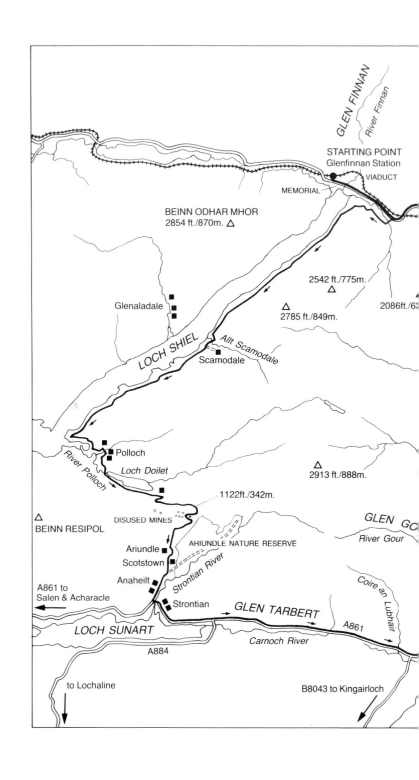

GLEN FINNAN

River Finnan

STARTING POINT
Glenfinnan Station

VIADUCT

MEMORIAL

BEINN ODHAR MHOR
2854 ft./870m. △

2542 ft./775m.
△

2086ft./6⁣

△
2785 ft./849m.

Glenaladale

LOCH SHIEL

Allt Scamodale

Scamodale

River Polloch

Polloch

Loch Doilet

1122ft./342m.

2913 ft./888m.
△

GLEN GO

River Gour

△
BEINN RESIPOL

DISUSED MINES

AHIUNDLE NATURE RESERVE

Ariundle
Scotstown

Anaheilt

Strontian River

Strontian

GLEN TARBERT

Coire an Lubhair

A861

A861 to
Salen & Acharacle

LOCH SUNART

Carnoch River

A884

to Lochaline

B8043 to Kingairloch

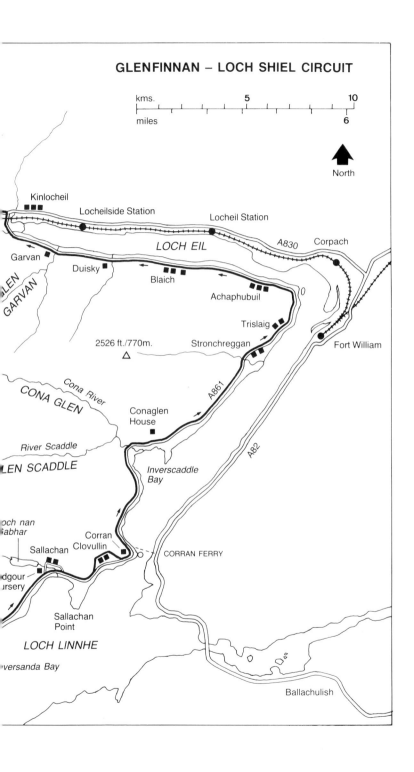

GLENFINNAN – LOCH SHIEL CIRCUIT

kms.   5   10

miles   6

North

Kinlocheil

Locheilside Station

Locheil Station

A830

Corpach

LOCH EIL

Garvan

Duisky

Blaich

Achaphubuil

Trislaig

2526 ft./770m.

Stronchreggan

Fort William

GLEN GARVAN

CONA GLEN

Cona River

A861

Conaglen House

River Scaddle

GLEN SCADDLE

Inverscaddle Bay

A82

och nan
abhar

Corran
Clovullin

Sallachan

CORRAN FERRY

dgour
ursery

Sallachan
Point

LOCH LINNHE

versanda Bay

Ballachulish

over rivers was won on April 1st, 1901, when the first steam engine arrived at the sea.

Leaving Fort William, the train passes the Nevis Distillery, crosses the River Nevis and then branches off to the left, skirting the shores of Loch Linnhe. To the right, by the banks of the Lochy, are the ruins of Inverlochy Castle, a stronghold of the Comyn family. On this site there once existed an ancient city and castle where the Pictish kings resided at intervals and where, in 790, King Achains signed a treaty with Charlemagne. This area was the scene of at least two important battles: in 1431 Donald Balloch and his clansmen defeated the forces of James I of Scotland, and on February 2nd, 1645, Montrose and his Royalist forces utterly routed Argyle and his army of covenanters at Inverlochy itself.

After Banavie, the railway line crosses the Caledonian Canal and continues to Corpach, where boats on their way to Inverness from Loch Linnhe pass through a remarkable series of eight locks, known as Neptune's Staircase, to reach the canal. The Caledonian Canal was engineered by the great Thomas Telford: started in 1803, it took nineteen years to complete.

At Glenfinnan, on the shores of Loch Shiel, some of the finest Highland scenery and history come together. At the head of the loch, a narrow strip forms the natural stage for the monument which commemorates August 19th, 1745, when Prince Charles Edward Stuart, Bonnie Prince Charlie, raised his Standard and heard his father proclaimed King James VIII of Scotland and III of England and Ireland. The monument, a 65ft column surmounted by the statue of a Highlander, was built in 1815 by Alexander MacDonald of Glenadale. Around it is an octagonal wall which commemorates in Gaelic, Latin and English "the generous zeal, the undaunted bravery and the inviolable fidelity of his forefathers and the rest of those who fought and bled in that arduous and unfortunate enterprise".

The story of the various attempts by the Stuart Pretenders to regain the throne lost by James II in 1688 is complex. Suffice it to say that the final one, the '45 as it is often known, came closer to success than any. That Monday, when the Prince raised his standard at Glenfinnan, he was supported by a thousand men from many different clans, some from as far away as Aberdeenshire. By December 4th that year, he and his assorted Highlanders had fought their way to Derby, a mere 100 miles from London. In the capital there was

panic: shops closed everywhere, all business was suspended, there was a run on the banks and George II packed his bags for a getaway. The crown seemed to be there for Prince Charlie's taking. But the promised support from the English Jacobites was not forthcoming and the Scots' nerve failed them. Two days later, shortly after dawn, they turned for home. The retreat continued into the Highlands and the final act took place in driving sleet on Culloden Moor, just outside Inverness, on April 16th, 1746, when the Prince and his now much-diminished army were totally overwhelmed by William, Duke of Cumberland.

Stinking Billy is what the Scots call the flower that in England is known, after Cumberland, as Sweet William — and with good cause. The brutalities of Cumberland's troops at Culloden were followed by systematic pillaging of the glens, leaving poverty and starvation where once there had been plenty. The ruthless pursuit of individuals, the show trials and executions in London, the 'abolition' of the kilt, tartan, weapons, even the speaking of Gaelic, together these effectively destroyed the ancient clan system and reduced Scotland to a state of vassaldom.

The Prince managed to escape capture, hiding in the Western Isles where he was sheltered by loyal supporters — Flora MacDonald famously risked her life for him — despite a price of £30,000 on his head, an enormous sum of money in those days. He finally sailed from Loch Nan Uamh via Loch Shiel back to France after which he spent the rest of his days working the capitals of Europe, a pathetic spectacle and dismal testament to the power of self-pity and the bottle. He died in Rome in January 1788. Like most lost causes, the Stuarts, and especially the Prince, have long since become the subject of romantic stories, embellished by songs full of sentiment and lies.

A very different history surrounds the area of Strontian, which in Gaelic has the delightful translation 'Point of the Fairies'. Lead was first mined here during the early eighteenth century by Sir Alexander Murray, a keen mineralogist who acquired the estates of Sunart and Adnamurchan. By 1729 the numerous storehouses, smithies, furnaces and workers' dwellings which had been erected around the original tiny clachan grew into the straggling townships of Anaheilt, Scotstown and Ariundle. They became known collectively as 'New York' after the name of the mining company to which they owed their existence. At their peak, the output of lead was said to be 600 tons and, in 1753, sixty tons was used in the roof of the new Inveraray Castle. But the mines ran into difficulty, technical and financial, and from 1769 they were operated only occasionally. The mineral strontianite, discovered in 1764, led to the isolation of the element strontium by Thomas Hope in 1790. This had no particular scientific importance until the nuclear age. Strontium 90, a radioactive isotope of strontium, is an important element in nuclear fall-out. Today only the mining of barytes has continued to prove financially viable.

At Scotstown a single-track road turns east to the Ariundle National Nature Reserve, established in 1977 and owned by the Nature Conservancy Council. The wood is a fine example of the broadleaf woodland which once covered most of the lower ground of the west of Scotland. In the clearings are old charcoal hearths left from the nineteenth century when iron ore smelting was an important industry in Scotland. The wood was also used for tanning and bobbin making.

The hills of Ardgour

Leaving Strontian, the route follows the shore of Loch Sunart (Sweyn's Fiord) for a couple of miles. This loch marks the border between Ardnamurchan peninsula to the north and Morvern to the south. In the twelfth century both Sunart and Ardnamurchan were in the grip of Viking rule and even after Norway officially ceded the Western Isles to the Scottish Crown in 1266, a cruel lord with the wonderful name of Muchdragon Mac ri Lochlann continued to hold this peninsula. He was eventually defeated by John the Bold who was rewarded for his efforts by King John Baliol with the much less romantic title of Lord Ardnamurchan.

Ardgour is the most highly mountainous area of this remote westerly region. Lifting abruptly and magnificently from the shores of Loch Linnhe, its hills extend eleven miles west to Loch Shiel. Access from the mainland to this peninsula is either around Loch Linnhe and Loch Eil or via the Corran Ferry, which operates at the entrance to Loch Linnhe. These narrows are only a quarter of a mile wide which causes an extremely fast tide race and although the journey now is short and safe, earlier this century the combination of the tide race and high winds would often be enough to sink the ferry. Since the fifteenth century, Ardgour has been held by the Maclean clan but over the years their property has dwindled and most of the land is now owned by sporting estates and the Forestry Commission.

Map: OS Landranger nos. 40, 41 and 49

Distance: 64 miles, 102 kilometres

Difficulty: easy

Time: one long day. When the weather is good it is worth taking two.

Logistics: by train to Glenfinnan or by car on the main A830(T) Fort William to Mallaig road.

Route description
13 miles (21km) track, 51 miles (81km) of tarmac.

Although this tour has a larger proportion of tarmac than track, much of the former is single-track road and the area is so remote that traffic is usually light. If you are travelling to Glenfinnan by train it is IMPERATIVE that you reserve space for your bike(s) with Scotrail/ British Rail. If you don't, they can refuse to let you on. There is

Watch out for logging operations

a steam train which leaves Fort William in the morning on weekdays and at midday on Sundays, but don't bother to get excited as Scotrail refuse to carry bikes on it and told me very curtly they would be keeping to this policy for the foreseeable future. Shame on them. All train information is available from Fort William station, telephone 0397 703791. There is a small new railway museum at Glenfinnan station which is worth a visit as it has some wonderful photographs of times past and present and also some excellent train-orientated postcards and posters. It is open all week including Sundays, 9.30 am to 4.30 pm.

At mile .74 is the Glenfinnan visitor centre and monument, both of which are worth a visit.

The track along Loch Shiel is wonderful − a good firm surface and not many steep hills! Much of the land is owned by the Forestry Commission who were logging when I rode it − it is wise to watch out for this before riding full tilt round a corner straight into tree trunks swinging across the track. At Polloch the surface returns to single-track tarmac and after the village is a *mega*-steep hill − check pacemaker before start! The pain of the ascent is soon forgotten with the following equally steep descent which, if you can see through the speed-tears, gives a panoramic view over Loch Sunart and the Morvern hills. Just before the bottom, at log mile 23.30, is a sign to Ciotach Crafts and Woodturning, a little shop full of wooden delights which is certainly worth the short uphill climb to its front door.

Turn left at the junction at the bottom of the hill and you come to Strontian, a small village but with all services. The single-track road becomes main road shortly after leaving Strontian, returning to single-track again 12.95m (21km) later at the Corran Ferry. Just before the ferry is the village of Clovullin. Its shop is limited but is open on Sundays from 11 am to 1 pm

After Corran Ferry the route follows the lochside and is a delightful, gentle ride past crofts and deciduous woodland. If you are not into camping, many of the farms along this route do bed and breakfast, although if you are touring in the high season it would be best to book ahead. The tourist office at either Strontian or Fort William (see page 106) can give you advice and information.

Route Log
00.00m (00.00km) Glenfinnan station, museum, hotel and gift shop.
00.03 (00.05) Turn left. Telephone.

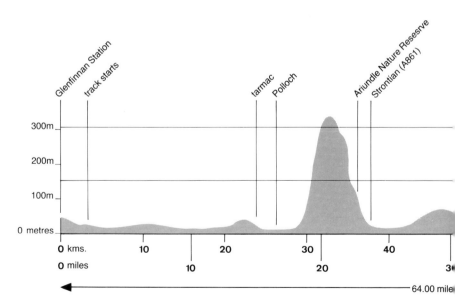

00.50 (00.80) Church, Our Lady at St Finnan.

00.62 (00.99) Glenfinnan House Hotel.

00.74 (01.19) Railway viaduct and the visitors centre on the left, monument on the right.

02.10 (03.40) Turn right, end of tarmac.

02.22 (03.57) Locked bar, easily negotiable.

02.24 (03.60) Junction, keep straight.

12.50 (20.00) Gorstanvorran House.

15.23 (24.40) Locked barrier, keep straight. Tarmac starts shortly after.

16.16 (26.00) Polloch. Junction, turn right and bear right again over the bridge.

16.41 (26.40) Keep straight.

16.64 (26.77) Bridge.

17.54 (28.22) Keep straight.

18.36 (29.54) Junction, keep right, start of the steep hill.

19.63 (31.58) Cattle grid − final assault.

19.88 (32.00) Summit.

20.35 (32.74) Strontian mineral mine.

22.18 (35.68) Telephone box.

22.78 (36.35) Junction. Left to Ariundle oakwood and Strontian river walks. If you have the time this is a pretty ride. The track

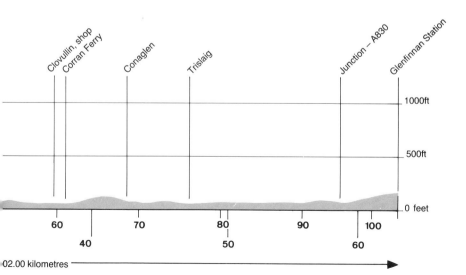

25

is good and the woods are marvellous (see area information). Otherwise keep straight.

23.81 (38.31) T-junction, A861, turn left for Strontian and Ardgour.

23.86 (38.40) Bear right. Shops, tourist office (also open on Sundays, 11 am-2 pm) and toilets on the left.

24.18 (38.90) Shop and post office (open Sundays, 11 am-5 pm).

25.65 (41.27) Junction, keep straight (right for Rahoy and Glensanda tours, see page 27).

31.92 (51.35) Junction, keep straight.

32.29 (51.95) Telephone box.

33.45 (53.82) The view looks straight up to the Pap of Glencoe.

37.10 (59.69) Turn left for single-track loop, shop.

37.72 (60.69) Telephone box.

38.00 (61.14) Rejoin main road.

38.60 (62.10) Lighthouse and Corran Ferry. (Alternative route back to Fort William via A82(T) − extremely busy road.) Hotel.

38.64 (62.17) Telephone box.

38.88 (62.55) Post office and shopette.

43.12 (69.38) Conaglen.

48.00 (77.23) Trislaig, Fort William on the opposite shore.

48.92 (78.71) Telephone box.

53.83 (86.61) Telephone box.

56.62 (91.10) Telephone box.

59.51 (95.75) T-junction (A830), turn left.

64.00 (102.00) Glenfinnan station.

3

Morvern Peninsula
Rahoy − Loch Sunart

For area information see pages 20 to 24.

Map: OS Landranger nos. 40 and 49

Distance: 28 miles, 45 kilometres

Difficulty: challenging

Time: one day

Logistics: by road from the A861 Corran Ferry to Strontian Road: at the head of Loch Sunart turn onto the A884 signposted to Lochaline.

Route description

9.81 miles (15.78 km) track, 2.45 miles (3.95km) steep trail, 15.74 miles (25.32km) tarmac.

But for the steep mountain ascent and descent in the middle, this tour would fall into the easy category. The Morvern peninsula is not on the general tourist map and this must be one of the few routes where you can let rip on a downhill without having to slow down too much for traffic. This peninsula has no large towns on it and the nearest services are at the village of Strontian − post office, general store, hotels and small tourist office (see Loch Shiel tour). The track is in good condition and the only really tough part is the one and a half miles over Beinn Ghormaig at Rahoy. This is definitely not one for flabby muscles − I had to carry my bike for most of this section. But the views from the summit over Loch Sunart and north to Ardnamurchan are well worth the sweat and the moans of ''are we nearly there?'' from your companions! Once over the forestry fence stile, you enter an enchanting world as the trail takes you down to Glencripesdale. The path wanders its way over soft peaty mounds covered in pine needles and a few soggy patches which slurp quietly as you fall into them − speaking for myself of course!

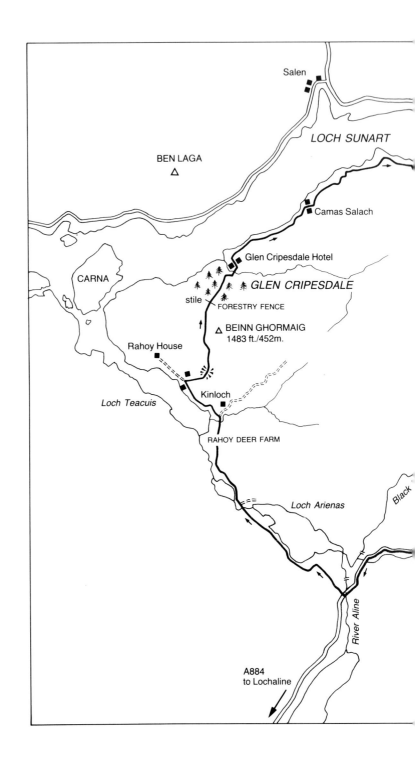

Salen

LOCH SUNART

BEN LAGA
△

Camas Salach

Glen Cripesdale Hotel

CARNA

GLEN CRIPESDALE

stile
FORESTRY FENCE

△ BEINN GHORMAIG
1483 ft./452m.

Rahoy House

Kinloch

Loch Teacuis

RAHOY DEER FARM

Loch Arienas

Black

River Aline

A884
to Lochaline

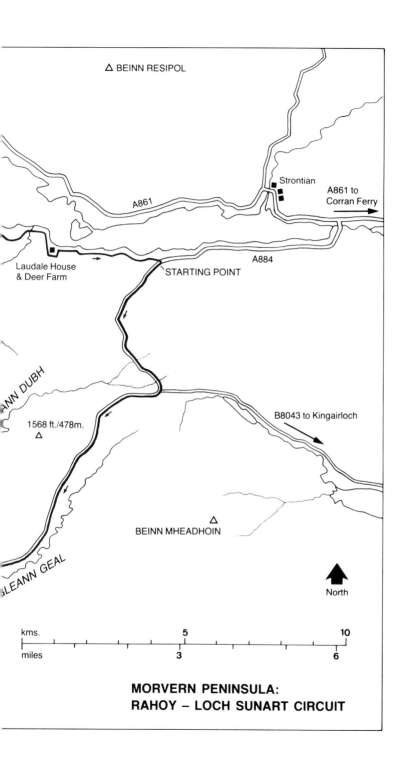

△ BEINN RESIPOL

Strontian

A861 to
Corran Ferry

A861

Laudale House
& Deer Farm

STARTING POINT

A884

ANN DUBH

1568 ft./478m.
△

B8043 to Kingairloch

△
BEINN MHEADHOIN

GLEANN GEAL

North

kms.
miles

5
3

10
6

**MORVERN PENINSULA:
RAHOY – LOCH SUNART CIRCUIT**

Glen Cripesdale Hotel

Looking west over Loch Sunart and Ardnamurchan

I felt most ungainly compared to the roe deer who sure-footedly danced away into the undergrowth, the flash of their white rumps sometimes the only giveaway that they had been there at all. If you are lucky, a pinemarten may scamper across your path. Glencripesdale Hotel, which you bike past at the end of the forestry trail, is the most delightfully remote hotel. They advised me that though they have only a residents bar, they would be pleased to

Enchanted woodland

An uphill slog

serve you a bar meal provided you let them know in advance — telephone 096785 263. The hotel is open from March 1st until the end of October. I can only advise you not to be put off by the hill-climbing section because this is a charming part of Scotland. Seeing the deer at Rahoy and Laudale is an experience not to be missed, and Loch Sunart is one of the most beautiful lochs on the west coast.

Route Log

00.00m (00.00km) Starting-point where track meets tarmac (see map). Route follows single-track tarmac road, A884, up steep hill.

01.82 (02.93) Summit.

03.23 (05.20) Keep straight, ignore turn on the left to Kingairloch.

04.50 (07.24) Summit, delightful downhill run with views across Morvern to the Island of Mull.

08.96 (14.41) Road runs next to river and through some pretty woodland.

11.27 (18.13) Junction, turn right signposted to Kinlochtearcus.

15.39 (24.76) Rahoy deer farm.

15.74 (25.32) Schoolhouse on the left, keep straight, track starts.

16.15 (26.00) Bridge and fork, keep straight.

17.15 (27.60) Turn right off track immediately past the burn with a modern house on your left. Now comes the real sweat! This 'path' is new because the right of way was removed when the estate was turned into a deer farm. It is accordingly indistinct and you will need to folllow the Ordnance Survey map closely. But this is not big country and the features to look out for are easily found. The distance from turning off the track to reaching the forestry stile is approximately one and a half miles. Because the mileometer was unable to register while I was carrying my bike for this section, the following log can be only an approximation.

19.50 (31.37) Trail rejoins track, turn left.

20.50 (31.30) Glencripesdale Hotel.

22.00 (35.40) Camas Salach.

27.00 (43.40) Laudale House and deer farm.

28.00 (45.00) End of track, back to A884 and starting-point.

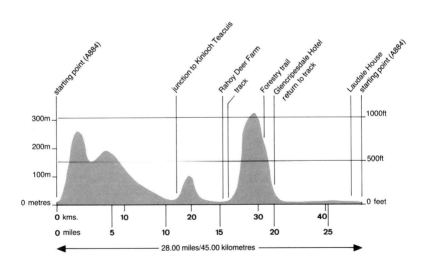

4

Morvern Peninsula
Ardtornish – Glensanda

For area information see pages 20 to 24.

Map: OS Landranger no. 49

Distance: 28 miles, 45 kilometres

Difficulty: challenging

Time: one long day

Logistics: by road from the Corran Ferry on the A861, turning off at the head of Loch Sunart onto the A884 road to Lochaline. If you are coming across from Mull, you catch the Fishnish to Lochaline ferry and thus onto the A884.

Route description
14 miles (22.50km) track/trail, 14 miles (22.50km) single-track tarmac road.

Well, this is some tour! Definitely not to be undertaken if you are unfit or like to bike only on smooth track. It is also inadvisable to do it after June because there is an abundance of bracken in the section after Airigh Shamraidh (log mile 11) which completely covers the trail and there is absolutely nothing more shitty or exhausting than having to thrash your way through bracken carrying a bike. Yes, I rode it at the wrong time! The other mistake I made was not taking enough water. When I rode this route it was well into a drought and after Glensanda the burns had all dried up. The burn water at Glensanda looks a dubious colour from all the quarrying but there are several houses and an office and I am sure they would not mind giving you a refill from their tap. When I bike here again I would certainly take more than one day (weather permitting of course), either by setting off in the evening and staying the night at the MBA bothy (log mile 3.75) and finishing the route the next day, or I would pitch camp at the ruins of Airigh Shamraidh. If you are planning

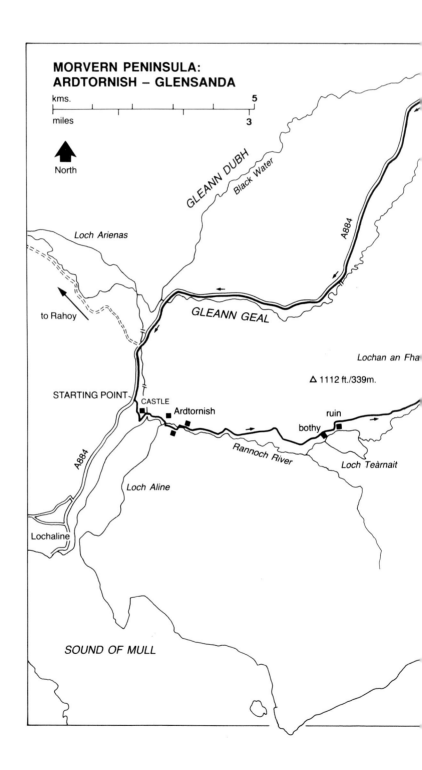

MORVERN PENINSULA:
ARDTORNISH – GLENSANDA

kms.   5

miles   3

North

GLEANN DUBH

Black Water

A884

Loch Arienas

to Rahoy

GLEANN GEAL

Lochan an Fha

△ 1112 ft./339m.

STARTING POINT

CASTLE

Ardtornish

ruin

bothy

A884

Rannoch River

Loch Teàrnait

Loch Aline

Lochaline

SOUND OF MULL

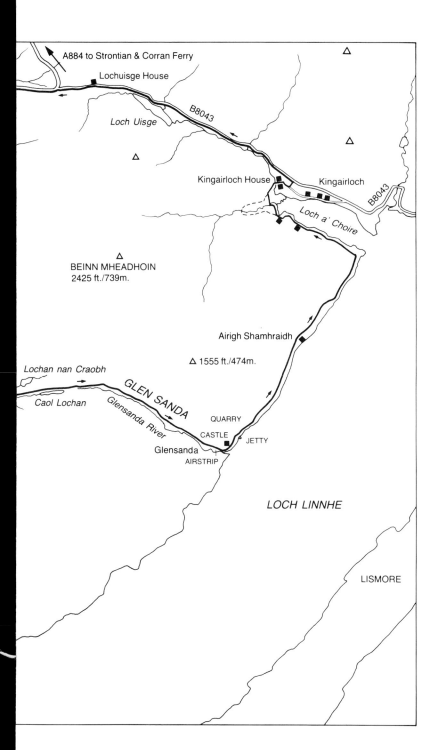

A884 to Strontian & Corran Ferry

Lochuisge House

B8043

Loch Uisge

Kingairloch House

Kingairloch

B8043

Loch a' Choire

BEINN MHEADHOIN
2425 ft./739m.

Airigh Shamhraidh

△ 1555 ft./474m.

Lochan nan Craobh

GLEN SANDA

Caol Lochan

Glensanda River

QUARRY

CASTLE

JETTY

Glensanda

AIRSTRIP

LOCH LINNHE

LISMORE

Bothy at Loch Tearnait

camping here for a day or two it would be worth taking your fishing rod. But of course if you are riding as an outward-bound biking test, then doing it in one day has the advantage of travelling light — a considerable advantage over this sort of terrain.

This is a tour of the most extraordinary contrasts. Setting off early on the most glorious sunny morning with the light catching the crystal water of the lochans and the occasional startled hare springing out from under the bike wheels, it seemed impossible to imagine that one of the most impressive quarrying schemes in Scotland was carving out the inside of the mountain Meall na h-Easaiche as I biked past. The company, Foster Yeoman Ltd, are quarrying granite on a grand scale, hollowing out the mountain from the inside and loading the rock onto a conveyor belt inside the mountain which carries it straight into ships which dock alongside. It is a curious sight to see the old, partially ruined fifteenth-century castle overlooking a Goliath of twentieth-century engineering. There are not a few that would wish the castle to have the power of David. But in its favour it employs about one hundred men who stay here and are ferried to and from the mainland by boat. When I rode this trail the sign at the quarry said blasting was between 4 pm and 6 pm and they prefer you not to be lurking in the area at that time. If you want to check the times, the telephone number is 063 172 489/521. If you get into trouble on this ride then I am sure they would help you out but this is not a ride to venture on without a full tool kit. The trail onwards from the quarry is a mixture of rock-hopping, pushing and carrying with bits of biking thrown in − good technical stuff! There are no services on this route: the nearest shops are either at Strontian or Lochaline and you'll need to organise accordingly. You have to cross a number of burns during the ride so I would not recommend it as a wet weather tour. Have I sounded too negative? I hope not. This remote corner of Scotland may be a far cry from the established tourist trails of the east coast or the big country of Torridon farther north and although the most testing and exhausting route I have ridden, the captivating atmosphere and seductive tranquillity of the hills and sea make it a very special place. I wouldn't have missed it for the world.

Route Log

00.00m (00.00km) Starting-point (see map), turn left at the turn-off from the A884 to Ardtornish.

00.33 (00.53) Keep left, signposted estate yard.

00.41 (00.65) Steps up to the old tower of Kinlochaline Castle. This is a partly restored fifteenth-century keep and is well worth a visit. You can pick up the key from the cottage next door.

00.46 (00.74) Bear right.

00.75 (01.20) Bear right and over little bridge. Ardtornish House and gardens on the left. Ardtornish is now let as holiday flats and the gardens are open to the public from April to October.

00.78 (01.25) Bear left.

00.83 (01.33) Walled garden, plants and shrubs for sale.

00.95 (01.52) Keep straight, through the farmyard.

01.02 (01.64) Bear left over narrow stone bridge.

01.03 (01.65) Keep straight.

01.07 (01.72) Three-way fork, turn right towards the white house.

01.15 (01.85) Fork, keep straight.

01.20 (01.93) Keep straight, start of grassy track.

02.00 (03.21) Watch out for deep peat puddle.

02.48 (04.00) Another cavern disguised as a puddle.

02.82 (04.53) Watch out for the bridge − it doesn't quite make it to the other side.

03.15 (05.06) Bog!

03.65 (05.87) Fork, keep left.

Fifteenth-century castle

03.75 (06.03) Loch Tearnait and MBA bothy.

03.93 (06.32) Ruin. Trail turns left and becomes no more than bent grass.

04.86 (07.81) At the fork in the burn, bear right keeping the right burn on your right hand under the shoulder of the hill.

05.87 (09.45) Caol Lochan on your right. In the next mile you will have to cross several burns.

08.00 (12.87) Rejoice! Gravel track and the end of the first cross-country section.

08.82 (14.19) Glensanda, keep straight.

09.00 (14.48) Glensanda Castle, information and map.

09.06 (14.57) Fork, stay left.

09.19 (14.78) Bear left up short brae.

09.25 (14.88) Bear right.

09.34 (15.00) At the bottom of the brae, bear right towards the cranes.

09.60 (15.45) Bike under an incredible mobile conveyor belt. If a ship is in dock and about to be loaded this is an operation worth watching.

09.70 (15.60) Bear right after the docking area.

09.80 (15.77) Tunnel into the mountain (not you!).

09.90 (15.95) Bear right along the coast.

10.00 (16.10) At the bottom of the brae, bear left by the white board and kiss goodbye to good track as it's back to cross-country.

11.00 (17.70) Airigh Shamhraidh (in Gaelic 'Shieling for Summer Grazing'). If you are thinking of camping on this ride then this is an enchanting spot, absolutely remote with a lush green field gently sloping down to the sea. The trail appears to continue along the shore but it is important that you bear left and follow the trail as shown on the OS map. I investigated whether the shore route was feasible but it eventually ends at a rocky cliff leaving you with an extremely stiff climb up to the map-marked trail.

13.48 (21.70) Cottage on the left. Trail improves considerably.

13.95 (22.45) Gate through wood, go over bridge and straight ahead.

14.10 (22.70) Gate, turn right past the farm.

14.15 (22.80) Gate and tarmac, continue past the houses following the road sharp right.

14.50 (23.35) Turn left up track through the wood.

14.75 (23.75) Turn left onto B8043, single-track tarmac road.

18.40 (29.60) Lochuisge – foxhound kennels on the right.

19.12 (30.80) Junction, turn left onto A884 signposted Lochaline, only one more small uphill and then a gentle, well-deserved downhill cruise back to Ardtornish.

28.00 (45.00) You made it!

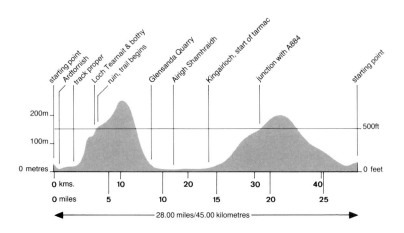

5

Aberfoyle – Loch Katrine

Area information

Loch Katrine is owned by the Scottish Water Board since, together with Loch Arklet, it forms Glasgow's main water supply. The Water Department also owns the two sheep farms around Loch Katrine (working a total of nine thousand sheep) and the S.S. *Walter Scott* which sails around the loch twice a day. This 115-ton pleasure steamer, built in 1900, is the only surviving screw steamer left in regular passenger service in Scotland. Sir Walter Scott (1771-1832) was Scotland's leading romantic author. He was born in Edinburgh and having been apprenticed to his father, a Writer to the Signet, was called to the bar in 1792. Despite the popularity of his romantic verse, he was eclipsed as a poet by Byron and in 1814 turned to writing novels at which he excelled. In 1820 he was created a baronet. Disaster struck in 1826 when the publishing firm he was involved in went bust and he lost everything. For the rest of his life he worked strenuously to pay off his creditors, all debts finally being met on

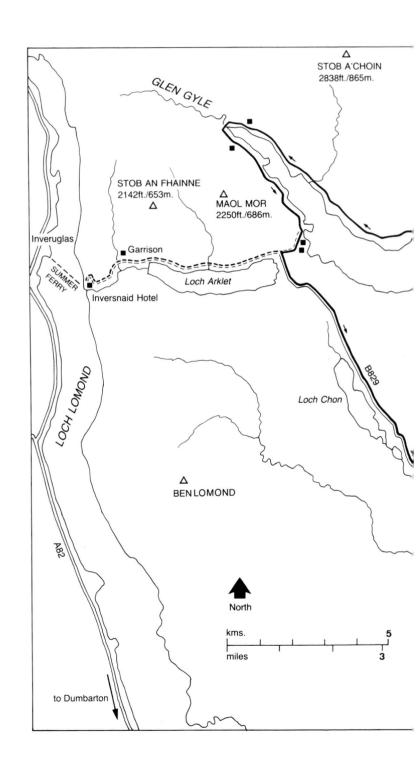

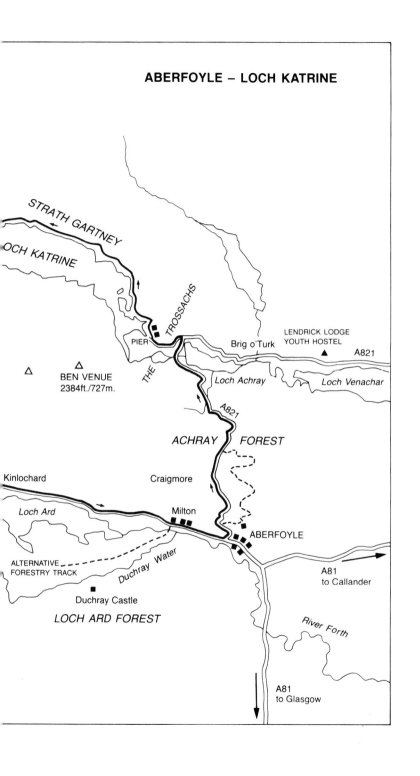

ABERFOYLE – LOCH KATRINE

STRATH GARTNEY

LOCH KATRINE

TROSSACHS

THE

PIER

LENDRICK LODGE
YOUTH HOSTEL

Brig o'Turk

A821

BEN VENUE
2384ft./727m.

Loch Achray

Loch Venachar

A821

ACHRAY   FOREST

Kinlochard

Craigmore

Loch Ard

Milton

ABERFOYLE

ALTERNATIVE
FORESTRY TRACK

Duchray Water

A81
to Callander

Duchray Castle

LOCH ARD FOREST

River Forth

A81
to Glasgow

his death. Rob Roy Macgregor was romanticised and immortalised by Scott although in fact his life story needed no embellishment at all.

Loch Katrine, Inversnaid and Aberfoyle are all situated in Macgregor country. *'S Rioghal mo Dhream'* − My Blood is Royal − is the motto of the Clan Gregor, who proudly claim their descent from the remnants of the ancient Caledonian nation. But despite their noble lineage (or maybe because of it), the clan's history is full of bitter fighting and persecution. The first recorded chief of the Macgregors of Clan Gregor lived around Glen Orchy, further north. But he fell foul of the Campbells and by dirty dealing and bribery was forced off his land. The Clan also suffered from Acts of Proscription, by one of which no more than four Clan Gregor members were allowed to meet together. (How this law was enforced in the middle of nowhere is quite beyond imagination.) They were also forbidden to wear swords. One Act even outlawed the name Macgregor and often the women were branded on the cheek. When Charles II was restored to the throne in 1660, he promised the restitution of Macgregor lands in return for the clan's part in the Royalist campaign. But it never happened and Clan Gregor alone among the sixty principal families of Scotland had no homeland.

The victimisation only served to increase the strong bonds between the members of the clan, and their expertise in guerilla warfare earned them the Gaelic name *Clann a Cheathaich* − The Children of the Mist.

Into this clan Rob Roy Macgregor (1671-1734) was born, the youngest son of Donald Macgregor of Glengyle from whom he inherited Inversnaid. The site of Rob Roy's family home at the head of Loch Katrine is no longer visible as it was submerged beneath the surface of the loch when the level was raised by the Water Board. Growing up around Loch Katrine, Rob Roy developed a knowledge and intimacy with the hills and glens which by all accounts was remarkable. His chosen profession was cattle droving interspersed with cattle stealing, general plundering and occasional manslaughter.

Cattle were very much the lifeblood of the Highlander in the seventeenth and eighteenth centuries and a man who knew the cattle business was much sought after. The Highlands of Scotland had a different code of morality from the Lowlands in that the Highland code excluded cattle when it came to theft, regarding them instead as communal property. Blackmail began its life in this trade, being protection money paid by farmers to prevent Rob Roy and his sort stealing their cattle. Of course the organised 'watches' were not above spiriting away one farmer's cattle while protecting another's! 'Mail' is the Scottish word for payment or rent, but the sense in which 'black' was meant is unclear — perhaps simply not white, i.e. less than pure. In any case blackmail may now be counted as Scotland's most widespread export, seeping into crannies that even whisky cannot reach!

In 1693 Rob Roy married Mary of Cromer and set up home at Inversnaid on the east shore of Loch Lomond, settling down to build up his droving business. By 1711 his lands were extensive and he was held in great respect by the clan. But disaster befell him. He had raised a loan of one thousand pounds (a vast sum in those days) to buy cattle in the north for fattening and re-sale in the markets of the south. Bills of exchange were entrusted to his chief drover, one Macdonald, who was despatched to bring in the stock. But the temptation proved too much for Macdonald who absconded. As soon as he learned of this, Rob Roy took off in pursuit but his flight was misconstrued and his principal creditors, amongst them the Duke of Montrose, moved quickly to take possession of his property. So, early in March, Rob Roy returned to find his house ransacked, his family evicted and himself outlawed. By the summer of 1713 he had established his family under the protection of the Earl of Breadalbane and resolved to take revenge on those who had ruined him — in particular Montrose. The tales of his daring feats during this time are numerous and his sympathetic treatment of the poor has often caused him to be compared to Robin Hood. Following the 1715 Jacobite uprising, Rob Roy found himself on the list of forty-nine names 'attainted of high treason' unless they gave themselves up within a year. So once again Rob Roy found himself fighting to save his home from the torch and his property from confiscation. It was soon clear that his very presence in the area was like a red rag to Montrose and brought danger to the entire clan, so he settled his wife and four sons with relatives on the shores of Loch Katrine and moved his own base of operations to Glen Shira (near Inveraray) under the protection of Campbell of Argyll, from where he could continue to plague Montrose from a safe distance.

The legend of Rob Roy Macgregor rose to new heights when, over the next three years, he was captured three times and each time managed to escape. In 1720 he built a house and settled in Balquhidder and in 1725 General Wade arranged a formal pardon for him. He

A MacGregor graveyard

died in his bed at Inverlochlarig, Balquhidder, on December 28th, 1734, and was buried in Balquhidder churchyard on New Year's Day 1735.

The road down to Inversnaid passes through much wilder country than around Loch Katrine. On your right just past the end of Loch Arklet (Loch of the Bend of the Slope) are the remains of the Inversnaid Garrison. It was built in 1719 to try and control the Jacobites after the 1715 rebellion. One of the first acts of the 1745 rebellion was its seizure by the Macgregors. Sir Walter Scott passed it in 1792 and found ''a garrison consisting of a single veteran . . . the venerable warder was reaping his barley croft in all peace and tranquillity; and when we asked admittance to repose ourselves, he told us we would find the key of the fort under the door''. In 1820 it was occupied by two women who kept ''a kind of inn'' in the ruins, but in 1828 Scott reported it totally in ruins.

Tumbling down beside the Inversnaid Hotel are the waterfalls of the Snaid burn, which have inspired many to poetry, most notably Gerald Manley Hopkins and William Wordsworth who passed through Inversnaid with his sister Dorothy on their first trip to Scotland.

Returning to Aberfoyle past Loch Chon (Loch of the Dogs), Ben Lomond (974m/3,196ft) is on your right, followed by Loch Ard and Loch Ard Forest, also known as the Queen Elizabeth Forest Park. Aberfoyle, which means Confluence of a Pool, is a very tourist-orientated village, not only due to its beautiful position but also because of the writings of Sir Walter Scott and the adventures of Rob Roy. Of course, all Rob Roy's *direct* descendants come over from America to gaze at their homeland and fantasize, from the inside of a bus, that they too could be such a hero — and why not? When I am panting up some intolerably steep hill I often fantasize about being in a bus. The lush oak woodlands on nearby Craigmore are semi-natural, planted to satisfy the tanning industry's demand for oak bark. There was also, for a short time, an iron-smelting industry using the birchwood for charcoal. This rapidly declined with the introduction of coke-smelting.

Map: OS Landranger nos. 56 and 57

Distance: 29 miles, 46.67 kilometres

Difficulty: easy

Time: one day

Logistics: by car on the A81 Glasgow to Callander road or the A821 Aberfoyle to Callander road. The nearest train stations are at Dunblane and Stirling.

Route description

29 miles (46.67km) tarmac. There are short track loops through forestry — see below in conjunction with map.

The OS map has track marked around Loch Katrine but in fact this has now been covered in tarmac by the Water Board so this is not a tour for the macho, muscle-bulging biker whose idea of pleasure is bunny-hopping down sheer cliffs and who only carries a spare helmet and underpants in his tool kit. The road is closed to public traffic and any disappointment at the absence of track is soon forgotten with the stunning beauty of this part of Scotland. Late May or early June must be the best time to ride this route. The azaleas and rhododendrons are in bloom and the miles of glorious woodland you pass through are redolent with the scent from acres and acres of bluebells.

The log starts at Aberfoyle and takes the A821 north, confronting you instantly with a hill — gradient 10% and approximately three miles to the summit. I rode the tour in this direction out of a preference for getting over any nasties early on, but of course the choice is yours. At mile 00.79 is the David Marshall Lodge and Forestry Visitor Centre. You can turn off here and follow the forestry route, returning to the tarmac at mile 1.81, 2.56 or 4.35 (trails marked on the OS map). At mile 6.00 the route turns left to Loch Katrine and a mile further on is the pier where the steamer leaves (tea room and gift shop). It sails two/three times a day and will take bikes if there is room. For full details, contact the Aberfoyle Tourist Office, telephone 08772 352.

From the pier the single-track road follows the north side of the loch. At mile 15 there is a delightful walled graveyard at the edge of the loch: the only inscription still legible is marked Gregor Macgregor 1699. At mile 19 is the junction — left to Aberfoyle, straight on to the Inversnaid Hotel. The round trip to the hotel is seven and a half miles and is well worth it if the weather is good for the spectacular views over Loch Lomond. In summer a passenger ferry can take you from the hotel to the west bank of the loch (bikes no problem) and you can also join the West Highland Way here.

From this junction the journey is pretty much downhill to Aberfoyle. The single-track tarmac unfortunately ends at Kinlochard — telephone box and very friendly Post Office and general store, open on Sunday. This log follows the main route back to Aberfoyle but there is an alternative route through Loch Ard Forest which brings you out at the centre of the village. With so many tracks in the forest you can choose how far you wish to bike before reaching Aberfoyle. The area around Duchray Castle is private. To enter Loch Ard Forest turn right at Milton (log 27.13) and from there the OS map has all the potential routes marked.

Aberfoyle has all facilities and the tourist office is more than helpful should you need any information on the area. In case you are eyeing up the track marked on the south side of Loch Katrine, a word of warning. This is NOT a right of way and the Water Board refused me permission to even walk along it let alone bike it, their (reasonable) argument being that the track is extremely rough, help or telephone a long way away and they would have to rescue you.

If you are looking for a delicious meal after your day's biking, you will find something a little special at the Braeval Old Mill Restaurant (08772 711). Dinner is a set price menu at £29.50 (at time of writing), orders are taken from 7 pm-9.30 pm. Although dress was generally 'smart but casual', the proprietor assured me there were no rules − jeans are fine. Booking is essential as such 'guid tackle' is scarce outside cities in Scotland.

Route Log

00.00m (00.00km) Car park, Aberfoyle. Turn left at the tourist office, head west along the main street.

00.12 (00.19) Turn right, A821, steep hill − now is not the time to remember you had a chest pain last week.

00.32 (00.51) Bowling club on the left (in case you are already thinking of a different hobby).

00.79 (01.27) David Marshall Lodge and Forestry Visitor Centre on the right. Alternative forestry route.

01.81 (02.91) Forestry Commission Wayfaring Course on the right, and first exit of alternative route.

02.12 (03.41) Cottage and track to disused mine works on the left.

02.56 (04.12) Forest drive and bicycle trail on the right − second exit of alternative route. Good area for seeing blackcock, grouse and birds of prey.

03.36 (05.40) Final summit.

04.00 (06.44) Leannach car park and walks.

04.35 (07.00) Last exit from alternative forestry route.

05.58 (08.00) Loch Achray Hotel.

06.00 (09.65) Turn left − signposted Loch Katrine.

06.84 (11.00) Car park, visitors' centre, gift shop and tea room. Follow tarmac, single-track road to the right of the pier.

11.50 (18.50) Grassy track on the left which runs along the lochside for half a mile.

12.34 (19.85) Track rejoins road.

15.00 (24.14) Graveyard on the left.

18.50 (29.77) Lodge and boat pier.

19.50 (31.38) Junction. Straight on for the Inversnaid Hotel, Loch Lomond and the West Highland Way. Turn left for Aberfoyle.

24.37 (39.21) Kinlochard. Post Office, general store and telephone box. End of single-track tarmac.

24.62 (39.62) Youth Hostel (Lochard).

27.13 (43.66) Milton, turn right for alternative forestry route, otherwise keep straight.

28.37 (45.65) Main street, junction, turn right for car park.

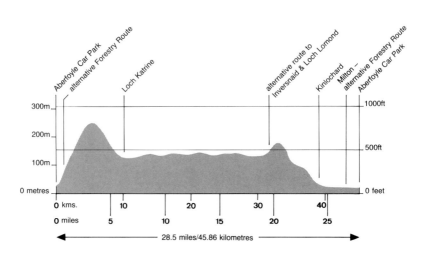

6

Pitlochry – Glen Tilt

Area information

In older times Pitlochry was a mere scatter of houses along the route between Inverness and Perth. Even by the early nineteenth century it had a population of only 334. Sheep fairs were held every August and horse fairs every May. Economic development of a sort began around 1738 when the larch tree was introduced into Scotland by a Mr Menzies of Culdares who brought a few plants back from the Austrian Tyrol. Five of these he left at Dunkeld and eleven at Blair Atholl for the Duke of Atholl. Although the then Duke recognized the qualities of this fast-growing deciduous fir, it was the fourth Duke who, after 1774, earned the title 'the planting duke' by planting some 15,573 acres of land with over 27 million trees, the largest part of them being larch. Since the native pinewoods in the area had suffered severe over-exploitation through the centuries because of the ease with which the timber could be floated down to the Tay, the Duke's was a sensible and far-sighted act.

When Queen Victoria visited Blair Atholl in 1845, she was accompanied by her doctor, Sir James Clerk, who thereafter recommended Pitlochry as an especially healthy district so that the town began to prosper as a health and holiday resort. By 1865 the Highland Railway had reached the town and thereby not only encouraged tourism but that other Victorian boom industry in Pitlochry – whisky distilling.

The appearance of Blair Castle, the residence of the Dukes of Atholl, has changed considerably over the past 250 years – storeys have been taken off, battlements and turrets removed and clock towers have gone up and down (the present one was erected in 1815). To the east of the castle there is a deep pool where reportedly, in days of yore, adulteresses were sewn up in sacks and thrown into the water to drown. Presumably the adulterer's part in this was of no consequence!

Glen Tilt is one of Scotland's major glens. At one time a much-admired marble of pure white, flecked with light grey and green,

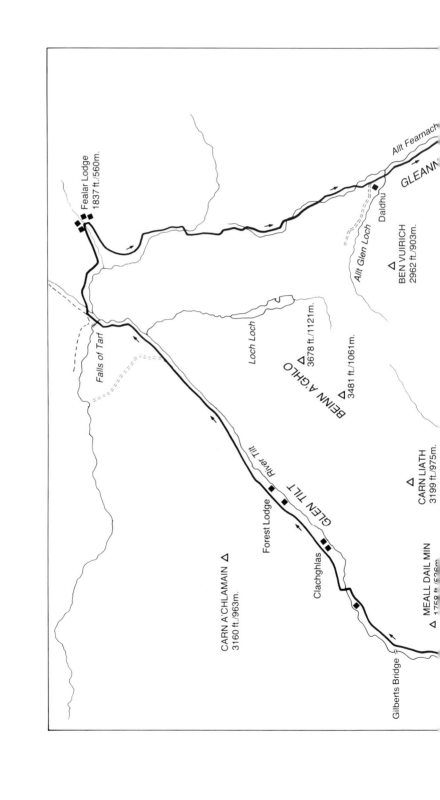

Fealar Lodge
1837 ft./560m.

Allt Fearnach

GLEANN

Allt Glen Loch

Daldhu

BEN VUIRICH
2962 ft./903m.

Falls of Tarf

Loch Loch

3678 ft./1121m.

3481 ft./1061m.

BEINN A'GHLO

River Tilt

GLEN TILT

Forest Lodge

CARN LIATH
3199 ft./975m.

Clachghlas

CARN A'CHLAMAIN
3160 ft./963m.

MEALL DAIL MIN
1759 ft /526m

Gilberts Bridge

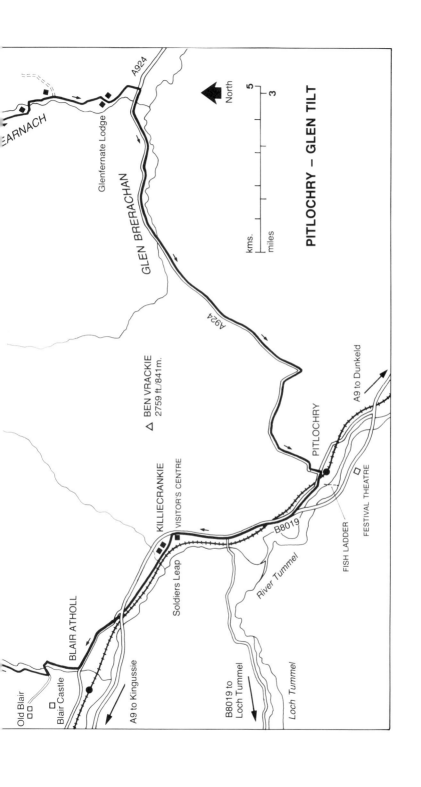

PITLOCHRY – GLEN TILT

North

kms.
miles

5
3

...ERNACH

A924

Glenfernate Lodge

GLEN BRERACHAN

A924

△ BEN VRACKIE
2759 ft./841m.

KILLIECRANKIE

VISITOR'S CENTRE

Soldiers Leap

B8019

PITLOCHRY

A9 to Dunkeld

FISH LADDER

FESTIVAL THEATRE

River Tummel

BLAIR ATHOLL

Old Blair

Blair Castle

A9 to Kingussie

B8019 to
Loch Tummel

Loch Tummel

The road up Glen Tilt

was quarried here. A less enviable aspect of the glen's past lies in its early association with the Clearances, that bloody and notorious episode in the early nineteenth century. In the case of Glen Tilt, however, the ground was cleared of its crofting families (it was once home to about five hundred inhabitants) not to make room for sheep, as was the case elsewhere, but for deer, animals which depend for their survival on access to low ground in winter.

Many of the men who lost their livelihood in this way were 'offered' alternative employment in the regiment which the Duke of Atholl was raising to fight in what my publisher, with an eye to American sales, calls the American War of Independence but which was technically a rebellion. Perpetual possession of a family's lands at the then existing rent was promised if they could raise a contingent equal to one man from each family. If there was any dissension then force was used. Although the Highlander's apparently mindless attachment to violence was deplored in peacetime, it was eagerly called upon when it could be put to work in the name of the Crown or Parliament! So bad was the endemic cattle-rustling in Scotland and so inefficient the English troops sent north to contain the lawlessness — they spent their time moping in their barracks, dreaming of a land without rain or midges — that the second Earl of Atholl was authorised to raise an independent company of clansmen 'to keep watch upon the braes'. These men were greatly feared and eventually became the nucleus of the most famous of all Scottish regiments, the Black Watch. When Queen Victoria was on one of her visits to Blair Castle in 1845, she was so charmed by the Duke and his tough Highlanders that she granted him the privilege of being the only British subject allowed to retain a private army, a right which is still exercised by the present Duke.

Finally, if you are driving past Blair up the A9, it is worth sparing a thought for the man, General George Wade, who, from 1726 onwards, engineered the framework of the present road system throughout the Highlands — much of the new main road is on the same line as his road of two hundred and fifty years ago.

Map: OS Landranger nos. 43 and 52

Distance: 45 miles, 72 kilometres

Difficulty: easy

Time: one day, but this is a stunning route and if you like camping in the wilds it is definitely worth taking longer.

Logistics: by train to Pitlochry, or by car via the A9 Perth to Inverness road or A924 Glen Shee to Pitlochry road.

Route description
22 miles (35.39km) of track/trail, 23 miles (37km) of tarmac.

This has to be one of the best routes in Scotland for mountain biking. Not only does it have an admirable track for riding on, surrounded by some of Perthshire's finest scenery, but the whole area is stuffed with interesting Scottish history (i.e. Blair Castle and Killiecrankie) and modern amenities (distilleries, Festival Theatre, restaurants, etc.).

If you are thinking of camping and cannot do without a hot shower and toilet, then there is a choice of campsites — one as you enter the town on the left and one at Faskally as you leave (see log route). On the other hand, if you are planning to camp en route, the choice of places is endless, each more tempting than the last, and of course finding fresh water is no problem. The track up Glen Tilt is in excellent order, a very gradual uphill gradient from approximately 150m at the start to 400m where track meets trail. Here the route is at its steepest, rising from 400m to 550m in one and a half miles. Although more technical than the track, it is still fairly easy. The

Fealar Lodge

trail ends and the track resumes at Fealar Lodge, reportedly the highest lodge in Scotland inhabited all the year round. The twelve and a half miles from Fealar Lodge to the A924 is a downhill doddle apart from one ascent between Gleann Mor and Carn an t-Sionnach (Cairn of the Fox to you and me). There was an abundance of deer, grouse and hares when I went through and I have no doubt that a leisurely ride would have revealed many more delights. Once onto the A924 take care since to begin with, the road is little more than single-track and certain drivers are inclined to behave as if bikers belong in the ditch. There is only one more long slow uphill before a superb speedy downhill into Pitlochry — watch out for a sharp corner halfway down!

Route Log
00.00m (00.00km) Pitlochry train station.
00.11 (00.17) Go up station entrance road to the main street and turn left.
01.05 (01.68) Keep straight on the B8019 (right turn for A9).
01.97 (03.16) Faskally caravan site and farmhouse accommodation.
02.66 (04.27) Junction. Keep straight on B8079 (left to Tummel Bridge and Kinloch Rannoch).
03.04 (04.89) Pass of Killiecrankie (National Trust).

03.75 (06.03) Killiecrankie Visitor Centre.
04.83 (07.77) Killiecrankie Hotel.
05.06 (08.14) Smell that cooking fat? Yes, it's a Little Chef.
06.68 (10.74) Blair Atholl.
06.98 (11.23) Shop — general stores, telephone.
07.00 (11.26) Junction, turn right — signposted Old Blair.
07.68 (12.35) Keep left over the bridge, ignore the sign to Deeside by Glen Tilt, walkers' path.
07.87 (12.66) Turn right by the gate lodge for Glen Tilt, start of track.
10.63 (17.10) Cattle grid, countryside opens out, Gilbert's Bridge on the left.
15.37 (24.73) Forest Lodge.
15.61 (25.11) Gate, metal stag in the field on the left.
17.68 (28.44) Waterfall.
18.02 (29.00) Ford.
18.76 (30.18) Fork, bear right.
19.50 (31.37) Track ends momentarily.
20.23 (32.55) Track becomes trail.
20.42 (32.85) Brilliant bridge and waterfalls.
20.61 (33.16) Fork, bear right.
20.66 (33.24) Cross the burn and start steep ascent.

River Tilt

21.40 (34.43) Follow the fence to the left.

21.94 (35.30) Gate, view of the lodge.

22.07 (35.51) Gate to the farmyard. Fealar Lodge.

22.14 (35.62) Bear right — track.

29.85 (48.00) Daldhu, end of track, start of single-track tarmac
 road.

33.03 (53.14) Beware of possibly closed gate to spoil downhill run.

34.02 (54.73) Glen Fernate Lodge.

34.18 (55.00) T-junction, bear left.

34.91 (56.17) Main road — A924 — turn right.

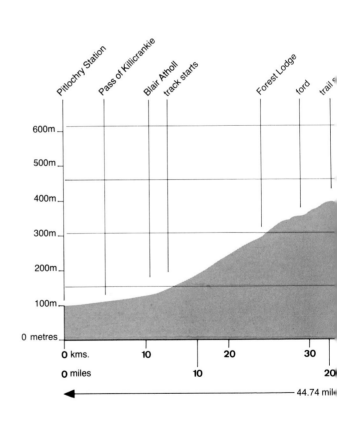

38.08 (61.27) Telephone box.
43.47 (69.94) Pitlochry.
43.82 (70.50) Post Office.
43.86 (70.57) Telephone box.
44.34 (71.34) Telephone box.
44.57 (71.71) T-junction. Turn right for train station, left for tourist information.
44.62 (71.80) Turn left for train station.
44.74 (72.00) Pitlochry station.

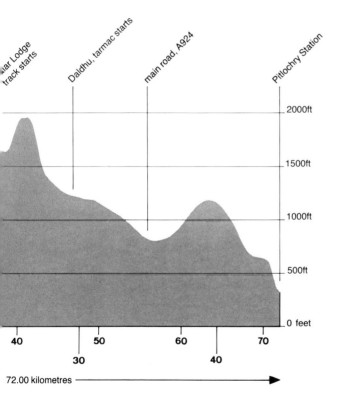

72.00 kilometres

Footbridge at the head of Glen Tilt

7

Ballater – Glen Muick – Balmoral

Area information

The first settlement in this area was at Tullich, about two miles east of Ballater, where two important routes crossed – that from east to west, Braemar to Aberdeen, and that from north to south, the Glen Muick road. Ballater was developed in the late eighteenth century as a spa for people who wanted to 'take the waters' at the wells of Pannich. For a long time there was no bridge over the Dee by Ballater and anyone visiting the wells had to cross the river by ferry. The present bridge is the fourth to be built, two of its predecessors having been destroyed by 'uncommon floods'. The present one was opened with great pomp and ceremony by Queen Victoria in 1885.

It was Francis Farquharson and his nephew who did much to develop Ballater – the name in Gaelic means Town of the Wooded Stream. Francis took part in the rising of '45 and led the Farquharsons at the battle of Culloden, where he was taken prisoner, conveyed to London, tried and condemned to death. Luckily he received a pardon and his estates, which had been confiscated, were returned to him on the payment of £1,613. When he died in 1790 his nephew William carried on the work of building the new village of Ballater which continued to grow, albeit slowly: by the 1840s its population was only 271. But its popularity grew as increasing numbers of people came to 'take the clean air' and enjoy the lovely scenery. Queen Victoria first visited Deeside in 1848 and from 1852, when Prince Albert bought Balmoral, the little town grew rapidly. In 1864 it held its first Highland Games which attracted 700 people.

In 1866 the railway from Aberdeen was extended to Ballater. It had been intended to continue the line along the Dee towards Braemar but Queen Victoria vetoed this idea. In 1886 improvements were made to the station, including a royal waiting room which was used by successive sovereigns for over one hundred years until the last Royal Train left Ballater on October 15th, 1965.

Originally Glen Muick (Muick is Gaelic for Swine) was covered

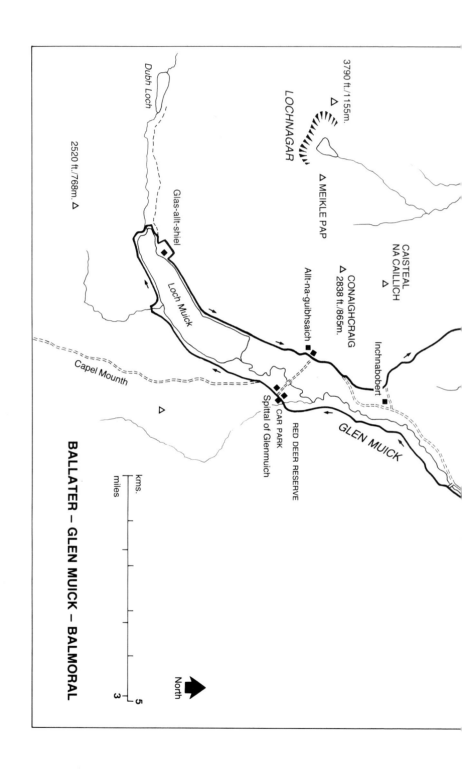

BALLATER – GLEN MUICK – BALMORAL

LOCHNAGAR
3790 ft./1155m. △

△ MEIKLE PAP

Dubh Loch

2520 ft./768m. △

Glas-allt-shiel

Loch Muick

CAISTEAL
NA CAILLICH
△

CONAIGHCRAIG
△ 2838 ft./865m.

Allt-na-guibhsaich

Inchnabobert

Capel Mounth

△

CAR PARK
Spittal of Glenmuich
RED DEER RESERVE

GLEN MUICK

kms.
miles

North

3
5

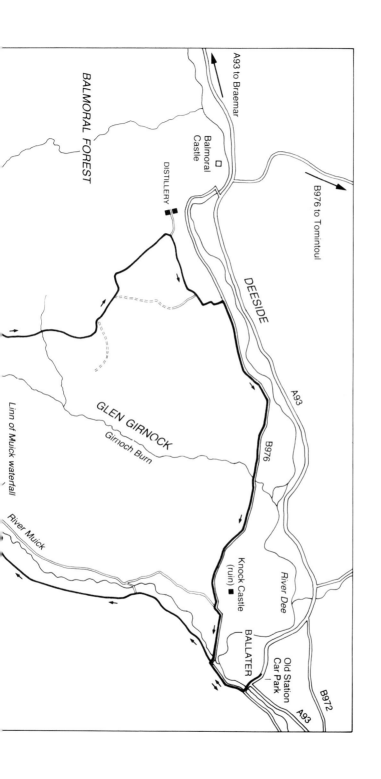

BALMORAL FOREST

A93 to Braemar

Balmoral
Castle

DISTILLERY

DEESIDE

B976 to Tomintoul

GLEN GIRNOCK

Girnoch Burn

A93

B976

Linn of Muick waterfall

River Muick

Knock Castle
(ruin)

River Dee

BALLATER

Old Station
Car Park

B972

A93

in Caledonian pine forest before a large crofting community settled there. A map of 1800 shows the cultivated areas as 'corn' lands: the mosses for cutting peat were numbered with each crofter having his own designated area. The Spittal (hospice or resting place) of Glen Muick was built as a staging post for the cattle drovers who used the track to take their beasts every season from the highland glens to the great lowland markets at Falkirk. It was also used for military purposes when cattle rustling and whisky smuggling were rife. Glen Muick was added to the Balmoral estate, along with Bachnagairn and White Mount, between 1947 and 1951 by King George VI. In 1974 Balmoral Estate, together with the Scottish Wildlife Trust, established the present nature reserve of 6,350 acres so that the land is now managed as a combination of working estate and nature reserve.

Queen Victoria's love for Scotland started when she first visited Edinburgh in 1842. Three years later she and Prince Albert stayed at Blair Atholl in Perthshire. Then, to make a change, they went further west to visit some of the islands which they thought positively enchanting – until it began to rain! The Queen at one time considered buying the great Ardverikie Estate on Loch Laggan but the constant rain changed her mind. Attracted by reports of the purity of its air and good climate, the Queen and her husband bought a lease of Balmoral in 1848 and in the autumn of that year arrived to take possession of a property which they had never seen. Such was their pleasure with the place that they opened negotiations for the purchase of the castle together with (let us be frank) as much of the surrounding land as they could lay their hands on.

As the Royal entourage grew ever larger, it was decided to rebuild the castle. For the job Queen Victoria chose William Smith, City Architect of Aberdeen, whose father had reconstructed the existing building for the previous owner, one Sir Robert Gordon. A new site was chosen one hundred yards to the north-west of the old castle which they could continue to occupy while the new one was under construction. The work was finished in 1856 and the old building was demolished. Prince Albert supervised the laying out of the grounds, the stables and the farms and, although he died before the work was completed, the Queen resolved that everything should go on as planned.

Queen Victoria loved Scotland and Balmoral and as years went by she spent more and more of her time north of the border. Her ministers were far from pleased that she was often 500 miles from the capital and those invited to stay at Balmoral were sometimes less than complimentary about the heating arrangements! The present Queen and her family are resident from August to October and on occasional weekends during the rest of the year.

The source of the River Dee lies in some small pools known as the 'Wells of Dee' which are high in the Cairngorms at a height of 4000ft (1220m). With a catchment area of only 825 square miles it is the smallest of the four big fishing rivers in Scotland (the other three being the Spey, the Tay and the Tweed), although some fishermen maintain that as a spring-fishing river the Dee is unsurpassable. The season opens on the first of February and with a cold winter and spring it is the lower part of the river which is initially better for fishing. The salmon move upstream as temperatures rise in April and May. There have been some huge spates on the River Dee, the largest being in 1829 when Thomas Telford's bridge at Ballater was swept away.

Glen Tanar has some of the finest Caledonian Pine forest on the east coast of Scotland. It is also similar to Glen Muick in that it is both a nature reserve and a working estate. The glen was bought in 1906 by the Coats family, who had made their fortune from textiles in Paisley, and in 1916 George Coats was made the first Lord Glen Tanar. His son Thomas died in 1971 and, having no male issue, the title lapsed with him. But his daughter, who married a descendant of Robert the Bruce, had a son and it is he who now manages the estate. Unlike some Scottish landowners, they have gone out of their way to come to terms with modern tourism and have made a fine job of integrating hill-walking and mountain biking into traditional activities.

Map: OS Landranger no. 44

Distance: Ballater – Loch Muick circuit, 25 miles, 41 kilometres
Loch Muick circuit, 8 miles, 13 kilometres
Ballater – Loch Muick – Balmoral circuit, 30 miles, 48.30 kilometres
Ballater – Glen Muick – Balmoral circuit, 24 miles, 38.60 kilometres

Difficulty: easy, although the eight-mile circuit round Loch Muick has some technical moments.

Time: one day per circuit. The loch Muick circuit is about two hours.

Logistics: by car on the A93 Aberdeen to Braemar road. The nearest train station is at Aberdeen.

Route description

Ballater − Loch Muick circuit: 8 miles (12.87km) track/trail, 17.40 miles (28km) tarmac.

Loch Muick circuit: 8 miles (12.87km) track/trail.

Ballater − Loch Muick − Balmoral circuit: 13.49 miles (21.70km) track/trail, 16.67 miles (26.82kms) tarmac.

Ballater − Glen Muick − Balmoral circuit: 7.44 miles (12.00km) track, 16.60 miles (26.70km) tarmac.

There is a selection of rides in this area. I have only logged the circuits but there are a couple more trails which lead to dead ends. Glen Muick and Loch Muick are run by Balmoral Estate and the Scottish Wildlife Trust as a wildlife reserve and while these circuits are open to bikers all year, the route over to Balmoral is not. As a rough guide it is closed from the beginning of August to the end of October when the Royal Family is in residence. For exact dates contact the Balmoral Estate Office − telephone 03397 42334.

The combination of routes to ride here is almost endless. I found the most fun circuit was the Ballater − Loch Muick − Balmoral one. It includes all the best contrasts for mountain biking without demanding a hairy chest. The single-track road from Ballater up Glen Muick rises from 656ft (200m) to 1,312ft (400m) over a distance of eight miles. The route around Loch Muick starts as track and after three miles becomes trail which lasts four miles. The trail is good in most places with, on one side for part of the time, a nice little sheer bank down to the loch to make falling off that much more fun. The last quarter of a mile of the trail is through a Caledonian Pine wood with some fun technical root-riding. Once out of the wood it is superb-quality track for the rest of the ride over to Easter Balmoral − hardly surprising as it has to be fit for a Queen! Where the track ends, the log turns right returning to Ballater but if you wish to visit the Lochnagar Distillery it is only a hundred yards or so down the single-track road to the left. It is open Monday to Friday 10 am-5 pm and on Sundays 11 am-4 pm; tours are free and there is a cafe where you can get refreshed. For information on when Balmoral

A track fit for a Queen!

Castle is open, ring either the Estate Office (number above) or Ballater Tourist Office – telephone 03397 55306.

The B976 South Deeside Road back to base is wider than single-track but very quiet with some fun little descents.

Because this area is a combination of wildlife and royalty reserve it is incredibly touristy so naturally it is much better if you can to ride out of high season (which is July and August).

The Loch Muick circuit is much favoured by walkers and I cannot emphasise enough the need for courtesy at all times. There are quiet rumblings of discontent about biking and it is up to us to make sure they get no louder. Are you listening, macho dickheads?

Route Log

00.00m (00.00km) Ballater. Car park next to old station. Tourist information office, restaurant, shops. Turn left onto main road.

00.20 (00.32) Junction, keep straight over the bridge, signposted South Deeside.

00.30 (00.48) T-junction, turn right, signposted Balmoral.

01.00 (01.60) Junction. Memorial to Queen Victoria and the Gordon Highlanders. Turn left before the bridge, signposted Glen Muick.

02.50 (04.00) Junction, keep straight.

05.20 (08.36) Sometimes amazing waterfall on the right.

05.90 (09.50) Cattle grid, route leaves forestry.

08.70 (14.00) Car park, Loch Muick wildlife reserve.

08.77 (14.11) Toilets on the right.

08.82 (14.19) Visitor centre, mega-binoculars to see deer with. Telephone.

08.86 (14.25) Junction. Log goes straight on around Loch Muick. If you are taking the shorter route to Easter Balmoral, turn right here, signposted Lochnagar path.

09.19 (14.78) Public footpath on the left to Glen Clova.

11.16 (18.00) Bridge. Pony path joins on the left (estate path, not a public right of way), track becomes trail, follow trail around the loch.

11.79 (19.00) Glas-allt-Shiel (the Shieling of the Grey Burn) opposite.

12.15 (19.54) Incredibly steep pony path on left. Keep straight.

12.69 (20.41) Trail joins the path from the Dubh Loch (Dark Loch).

12.73 (20.48) Although on the Ordnance Survey map the trail is marked going straight on, the Loch Muick circuit and this route log turn left here towards the pine wood.

12.77 (20.54) Once over the wall into the wood, turn left.

12.86 (20.69) Bridge (rotten at the time of writing so you may prefer to cross higher up).

13.00 (20.91) Junction with the track, turn left.

14.76 (23.74) Boathouse, alternative way back to car park and Ballater.

15.66 (25.19) Allt-na-Guibhsaich (Burn of the Scots Pine), junction. For another way back to the car park and Ballater turn right here. Keep straight for log route to Easter Balmoral.

16.15 (26.00) Take left fork into the wood.

16.86 (27.12) Lodge drive joins track.

17.66 (28.41) Ponyman's shelter.

19.45 (31.30) Rough track goes off to left, keep straight.

20.47 (39.93) Bovaglie Farm drive joins on the right.

20.75 (33.38) Summit, magnificent views towards Balmoral and the Cairngorms.

20.91 (33.64) Grouse butt on the left.

22.10 (35.55) You can see Lochnagar Distillery on the left.

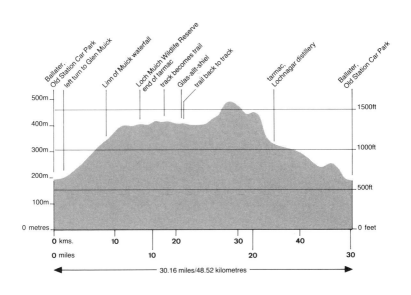

22.19 (35.70) End of track, tarmac. Junction, left for the distillery, log goes right back to Ballater.

23.61 (38.00) Junction, turn right for Ballater. Telephone box.

26.25 (42.23) Telephone box.

28.29 (45.51) Junction, keep straight. (Steep track on the left to ruin of Knock Castle if you need a quick thigh burn.)

29.16 (46.91) Bridge of Muick, junction with Glen Muick, bear left retracing route to Ballater.

29.86 (48.00) Junction, turn left over bridge.

30.16 (48.52) Car park, back to base.

8

Ballater – Glen Tanar

For area information see pages 63 to 70.

Map: OS Landranger no. 44

Distance: 25 miles, 40.22 kilometres

Difficulty: moderate

Time: one day

Logistics: by car on the A93 Aberdeen to Braemar road. The nearest train station is Aberdeen.

Route description
14.62 miles (23.52km) track, 10.38 miles (16.70km) of tarmac.

This is a very bonny route, starting in a relaxed fashion along the deserted railway, then crossing the River Dee over the iron bridge at Cambus O'May (Crook of the Plain) and continuing along the B976 to Glen Tanar. Once there, it is possible to do several rides of varying lengths and interest on tourist routes provided by the estate. Information on all activities and routes is contained on a large buff-coloured card, *Guide to the Waymarked Walks in Glen Tanar*, available from the tourist office in Ballater. Once the logged route leaves the estate buildings and starts through the Caledonian Pine forest, it is steadily uphill until log mile 15.40 when it becomes a steep uphill – 689ft (210m) in under two miles. When I biked this route the ground was very dry but it looked like there could be a nasty boggy area at the section called Black Moss on the OS map.

If you bike this tour in September you may see very bright blue blotches at various intervals on the track. These are grouse pellets (or shit if you prefer the Latin) after they have been feeding on blaeberries. The track is not so pristine for the descent and becomes very rubbly for a while near the bottom. Although most of it is 'easy' I have marked it as moderate because such a large percentage is uphill and the descent precarious in places. It is not suitable for young children.

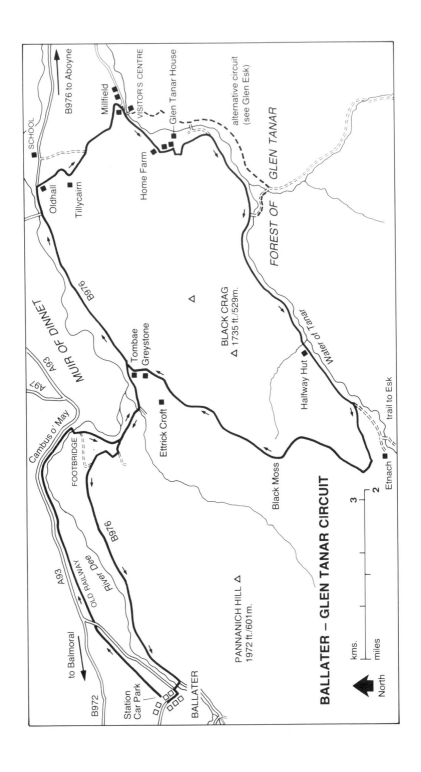

BALLATER – GLEN TANAR CIRCUIT

North

kms.

miles

0 1 2 3

B976 to Aboyne

SCHOOL

VISITOR'S CENTRE

Glen Tanar House

Millfield

alternative circuit
(see Glen Esk)

Home Farm

Oldhall

Tillycairn

FOREST OF GLEN TANAR

MUIR OF DINNET

A93

A97

Cambus o' May

B976

Tombae

Greystone

BLACK CRAG
△ 1735 ft./529m.

Ettrick Croft

FOOTBRIDGE

Water of Tanar

Halfway Hut

Black Moss

trail to Esk

Etnach

OLD RAILWAY

River Dee

B976

A93

to Balmoral

B972

Station Car Park

BALLATER

PANNANICH HILL △
1972 ft./601m.

Caledonian Pine forest in Glen Tanar

Route Log

00.00m (00.00km) Car park and railway station.

00.15 (00.24) Go straight across road, signed Ballater to Cambus O'May walkway.

01.22 (01.96) Cross main road.

01.90 (03.25) Straight across farm drive.

03.62 (05.82) End of railway, turn right over stile and then bear left along riverside path.

03.72 (05.98) Gate, must be closed after you.

03.81 (06.13) Turn right at bridge over the Dee. Excellent pool for swimming in. Awkward gates at each end of the bridge which you have to lift your bike over. Keep straight after the bridge through the trees to the gate. After the gate bear right and follow the track.

04.11 (06.61) Track continues along the left side of wood. Gate.

04.31 (06.93) Gate − electric fence in operation at the time of writing.

04.34 (06.98) T-junction, turn left on birchwood trail.

04.40 (07.08) Junction, keep left.

04.48 (07.20) Gate, end of track, turn left on road.

08.14 (13.10) Keep straight, on the left is the turning to Dinnet – one-horse town with pub, post office, general stores, Scots pines and toffs.

08.48 (13.64) Turn right, small sign to Tillycairn, Rowan Cottage. Track starts. Don't worry if you miss this turning as there is another a few yards down the road with the official right of way sign – they join after a short distance.

09.03 (14.52) Junction, keep straight, Tillycairn farm on the right.

09.25 (14.88) Junction, keep straight – check out carved stone on the left.

09.30 (14.96) Track off to the left, keep straight – another carved stone dated 1645.

09.53 (15.33) Junction, keep straight.

09.60 (15.44) Stone gateway, end of track.

10.12 (16.28) Junction with single-track road, turn right.

10.20 (16.41) Glen Tanar Visitor Centre on the left over the bridge, exhibitions and information on walks, trekking, etc. Possible alternative route for approximately two miles – see Glen Esk–Glen Tanar map (page 78). Log keeps straight on.

10.80 (17.37) Bear right, Glen Tanar House straight on.

10.87 (17.49) Riding centre on the left (in case you want to change your mode of transport).

10.92 (17.57) At the top of the brae, junction – bear left.

10.96 (17.63) Turn right, signposted to Glen Esk.

11.04 (17.76) Bear left following the right of way sign, past the keeper's house and through the gate.

11.12 (17.89) Track junction, go left following the right of way sign.

11.23 (18.06) Crossroads, bear right following the right of way sign.

11.57 (18.61) Keep straight, right of way sign.

12.31 (19.80) Track goes off to the right.

12.73 (20.48) Bridge, keep straight, alternative route joins here.

14.57 (23.44) Half-way hut.

15.40 (24.77) Junction, bear right.

16.20 (26.06) Junction, bear right – steep climb ahead.

16.36 (26.32) Grouse butts on the left.

17.36 (27.93) Summit, stunning views over Deeside.

17.80 (28.64) Potential bog. Saw a peregrine here.

17.87 (28.75) Gate, end of Glen Tanar reserve.

19.56 (31.47) Gate, electric fence at the time of writing.

19.79 (31.84) Keep straight, lovely farmhouse on the left.
19.98 (32.14) Junction, turn left back onto south Deeside road.
21.51 (34.60) Turning to bridge if you want to return via the railway. Log keeps straight.
22.81 (36.70) Pannannich Wells and Inn.
24.54 (39.48) Turn right over the bridge to Ballater.
24.66 (39.67) Junction, keep straight.
25.00 (40.22) Car park and railway station.

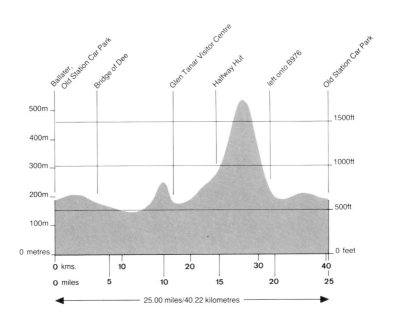

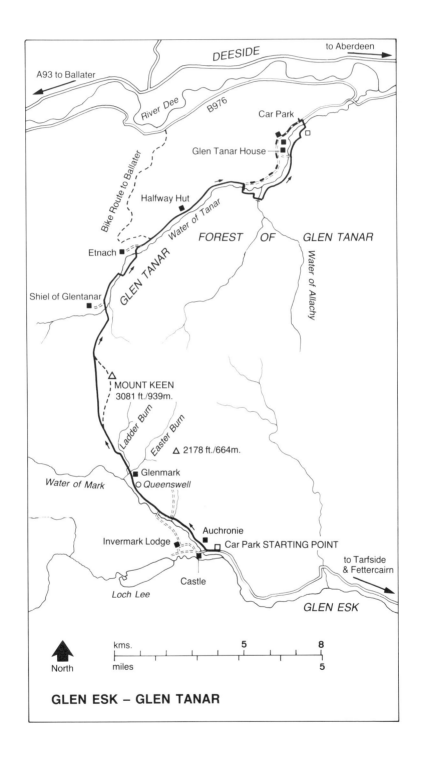

DEESIDE

to Aberdeen

A93 to Ballater

River Dee

B976

Car Park

Glen Tanar House

Bike Route to Ballater

Halfway Hut

Water of Tanar

FOREST OF GLEN TANAR

Etnach

GLEN TANAR

Water of Allachy

Shiel of Glentanar

△ MOUNT KEEN
3081 ft./939m.

Ladder Burn

Easter Burn

△ 2178 ft./664m.

Glenmark
○ Queenswell

Water of Mark

Auchronie

Invermark Lodge

Car Park STARTING POINT

to Tarfside
& Fettercairn

Castle

Loch Lee

GLEN ESK

kms.   5   8

North

miles   5

GLEN ESK – GLEN TANAR

9

Glen Esk – Glen Tanar

For area information see pages 63 to 70.

Map: OS Landranger no. 44

Distance: 15 miles, 24 kilometres

Difficulty: moderate

Time: half a day to a whole day, depending on your schedule.

Logistics: by car to Glen Esk. The Glen Esk road leaves the B966 Brechin to Fettercairn road near Edzell. The nearest train stations are Montrose and Stonehaven

Route description

14.87 miles (23.92km) track/trail, 00.13 miles (00.20km) tarmac.

It would not be advisable to ride this route during or after heavy rainfall as there are a couple of fords which could become seriously troublesome. Neither would it be wise if the mist or cloud is low since the turning near the summit is not clear and there is a misleading track, the extent of which is not truly represented on the OS map. But, adverse weather conditions apart, this is an absolutely brilliant ride although since it's not on a circuit you will have to beg, steal or borrow someone to drop you off at Glen Esk and collect you at Glen Tanar. The first half mile of this route is easy track, changing to superb wide trail for a mile then returning to track again until near the summit of the mountain. There you have a choice of trail: if you are revoltingly fit or just feeling masochistic you can bike right over the summit of Mount Keen 3,081ft (939m). I felt neither on the day so the log follows the slightly lower trail (a mere 2,461ft or 750m). Where the trail leaves the track (log mile 04.21), it's a bit messy with many little trails but if you keep to the left-hand side it gradually narrows down into the main route. It is approximately five miles from the car park in Glen Esk to the highest point of this ride which leaves ten glorious miles of downhill – but hang onto your hat, pants and anything else you treasure as the

Glen Tanar and Mount Keen

first section is pretty rugged down to 1,312ft (400m). Once into Glen Tanar the track is a veritable motorway sweeping you effortlessly through the Caledonian Pines, scattering endangered species and frightened walkers before you. No, I just made that up, but it's a great run!

Route Log
00.00m (00.00km) Glen Esk, car park.
00.13 (00.20) Turn right before the bridge, signposted public footpath to Ballater. Track starts.
00.23 (00.37) Bear left in front of the house, signposted to Mount Keen.
00.66 (01.06) Big iron gate, track changes to wide gravelled trail.
00.68 (01.09) Small ford.
01.17 (01.88) Ford burn.
01.19 (01.91) Track joins on right, trail ends.
01.41 (02.26) Junction with track from the lodge, keep straight.
02.00 (03.21) Yep, Queen Victoria was here too.
02.53 (04.07) Grassy track off to the left, keep straight on past the house.

02.70 (04.34) House on the right, start of the climb.

02.75 (04.42) Ford, could become quite deep in a spate.

02.86 (04.60) Ford — another one that could be troublesome after heavy rainfall.

04.21 (06.77) Stone cairn on the left of the track, turn right as if taking the trail to the summit of Mount Keen, keep to the left side and you will see where the trail round the summit leads off. Do not keep straight on the track as it leads only to grouse butts.

06.26 (10.07) Trail becomes very steep rough track.

07.01 (11.27) Wooden bridge, magic green field (for feeding deer in winter).

07.11 (11.43) Start of the good track.

08.69 (14.00) Track from Etnach joins main track.

09.28 (14.93) Track from Ballater — Glen Tanar route joins main track.

12.03 (19.35) Turn right over stone bridge, alternative route straight on.

12.34 (19.85) Track on the right, keep straight.

12.49 (20.09) Cross bridge and turn left.

13.95 (22.44) Crossroads, keep straight through the gate.

14.33 (23.05) Chapel, turn left.

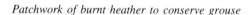

Patchwork of burnt heather to conserve grouse

Mountain Biking in the Scottish Highlands Vol. 2

14.41 (23.18) Bear right at the chapel and then left under the trees, keeping the building on your left.

14.64 (23.55) Track changes from gravel to grass.

14.83 (23.86) Turn left through the gate and over the bridge for the car park. Braeloine Information Centre in wee cottage ahead.

15.00 (24.13) Glen Tanar car park.

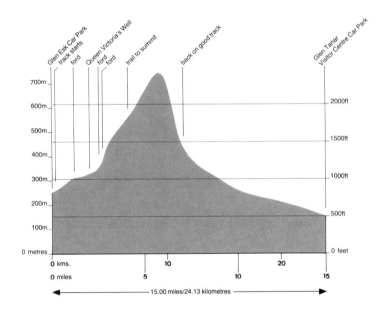

10

Aviemore
Glen More – Abernethy – Rothiemurchus

Area information

Originally Aviemore (in Gaelic, Big Hill Face) was a staging post
for horse-drawn traffic on the King's Road north. With the arrival
of the railway in the 1880s, it became an important railway junction
and the community grew accordingly, both in size and appetite –
'The whole district was tenanted by the navvies engaged in railway
work, who occasionally compelled the innkeeper to close his house
altogether and put up the shutters. In default of this concession it
was their playful habit to break all his windows. . . .'

In the late 1950s it changed again, some would say for the worse.
Two major projects incorporating some truly atrocious architecture
were the cause: the building of the first large-scale mechanised ski

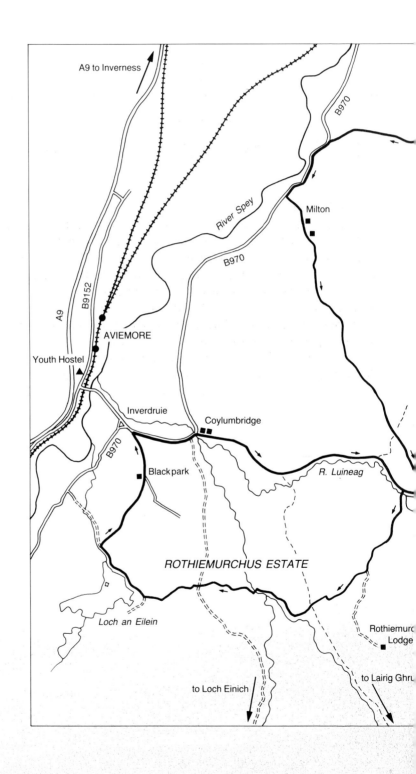

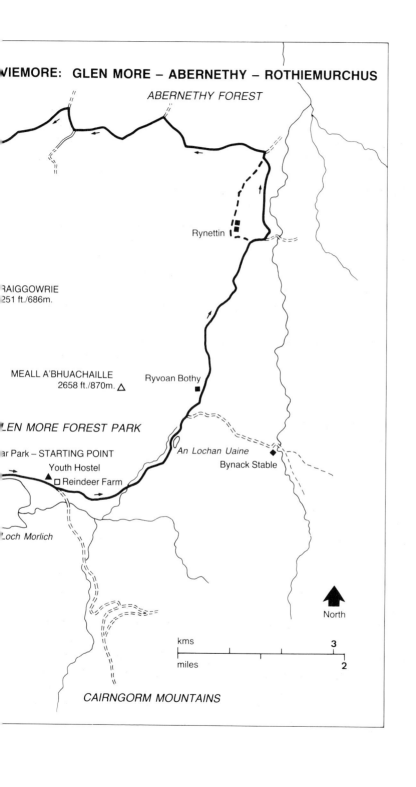

AVIEMORE: GLEN MORE – ABERNETHY – ROTHIEMURCHUS

ABERNETHY FOREST

Rynettin

CRAIGGOWRIE
2251 ft./686m.

MEALL A'BHUACHAILLE
2658 ft./870m. △   Ryvoan Bothy

GLEN MORE FOREST PARK

Car Park – STARTING POINT
Youth Hostel   *An Lochan Uaine*
▲ □ Reindeer Farm   Bynack Stable

Loch Morlich

North

kms   3
miles   2

CAIRNGORM MOUNTAINS

facility in Britain which opened in 1961, and the completion of the Aviemore Leisure Centure in 1966. It was quite a gamble at the time but one that paid off as Aviemore has since become Scotland's most popular tourist resort. The main reasons for the town's prosperity are the Cairngorm Mountains, which contain the majority of peaks over 4,000ft (220m) in Scotland, and a high plateau of a size unmatched anywhere else in Britain. Ecologically, the Cairngorms (Blue Cairn) is the most important mountain area in the British Isles, and indeed is of international significance. The area contains some of the finest and most extensive examples of mountain wildlife habitat in Britain, besides many geomorphological features representing important stages of the earth's evolutionary history. There is only one other place in the world (Baffin Island, in Canada) where you can see so clearly selective glacial erosion.

The lower ground contains important habitats for wild birds and one of the largest areas of native Caledonian forest in Scotland. To safeguard these features, much of the Cairngorms has been classified as a Site of Special Scientific Interest and in 1990 the British government announced its intention to nominate them as a World Heritage site.

The Cairngorms offer considerable opportunities for outdoor recreation. In most places, pressure is not yet excessive but in some areas there are problems with footpath and other types of erosion and recent trends such as mountain biking add a new dimension to the issue.

There can be no doubt that Rothiemurchus estate is one of the best examples of a deer forest that has integrated the needs of the tourist with those of traditional land management. In Gaelic the name Rothiemurchus means the Plain of the Great Pine and it still has large areas of naturally regenerating Caledonian Pine forest together with lowland pine and birch. It was owned by the Comyns, Clan Chattan and the Gordons before coming into the hands of Patrick Grant of Muckerach, second son of Chief of Grant, in 1574. A descendant of his, Ulysses S. Grant, commanded the victorious Union forces during the American Civil War and became President of the United States in 1868. The present Laird, John Grant, has the challenging task of running a modern estate, balancing tradition, conservation and commercialism. Naturally I am biased in thinking he does a magnificent job as he is a great supporter of mountain biking and hosts the mountain bike championships every year.

The estate is also brilliant for bird-watching, especially the osprey. Persecuted almost to extinction in the Highlands by 1920, it was not until the late 1950s that ospreys returned to Speyside. A little-known factor in their continued population expansion has been the ready supply of rainbow trout in fish farms. From mid-April to August you can frequently see these magnificent birds plunging in and carrying away a trout at Rothiemurchus fish farm.

Glen More Forest was bought by the Forestry Commission in 1923 and established as a forest park in 1948. Before that it was owned by the Dukes of Gordon, a family whose estates at one time stretched from sea to sea, from Speymouth to Fort William. Glen More is an area full of legends of ghosts and fairies. In particular, fairies are said to dance on moonlit nights around the little conical hill just above Lochan Uaine (Green Loch, log mile 03.12). Once a wandering shepherd stole their tiny fairy bagpipes but when dawn came he found himself holding nothing more than a puff ball to which a few blades of grass were attached. At mile 01.32 is the chance to pet a furry reindeer. In 1952 a herd of these animals was established here by Mikel Utsi. They came from Norrbotten in Sweden, travelling over a thousand miles by lorry, train, boat and horse-box. In 1961 a bull and some cows were brought from southern Norway, along with a young bull from Whipsnade − the offspring of a Russian reindeer — to prevent inbreeding. The herd has now stabilised at around one hundred head and is shepherded by a single person for most of the year. Unfortunately reindeer are very vulnerable to human interference — if one becomes separated from the main herd it may well pine away. At least six reindeer a year die from eating litter left by tourists (it becomes stuck in their throats) or from being worried by dogs. Mountain biking is another growing cause of disturbance. For information on accompanied visits to see the herd contact Alan and Elizabeth Smith, The Reindeer Centre, Glenmore, telephone 0479 861228.

Abernethy Estate is also now a nature reserve; I say 'now' but in fact it has been one since 1882. It is famous for its trees, bird life (you will find the Crested Tit here), wildcats and red squirrels.

A word about these shy and utterly delightful creatures: they are being steadily driven out of their traditional habitat by their cousins the grey squirrel (a relatively recent introduction to the UK) and at the present rate will soon be an endangered species. The grey squirrel is not the cuddly little thing you may imagine. It is a vicious bully which, besides terrorising its red brethren, kills hardwoods — by eating their bark — as if there was no tomorrow and should be treated like the rat it really is. So if you see one on the road, do not slow down (unless you have a chance to get two).

Map: OS Landranger no. 36

Distance: 29 miles, 46 kilometres

Difficulty: easy

Time: one day

Logistics: the nearest train station is at Aviemore. By car via the A9 Perth to Inverness highway (watch out for speed traps), B9152 (old road, runs parallel to A9), or B970 Kingussie to Grantown-on-Spey

Route description

17.16 miles (27.60km) of track, 11.84 miles (19.05km) of tarmac.

This route is in a figure-of-eight with the car park in the middle so, if you have no desire to do the whole tour, either of the loops is possible on its own. They are each excellent in their own right but the two together make a first-class biking day. The first loop through Glen More Forest and Abernethy Forest is all track with

Biking – a game the whole family can play

approximately four miles of tarmac. Apart from a couple of rubbly sections early on, the track is in good condition. The steepest uphill section starts just after you turn off the tarmac but it is not too crucial on the thighs. In fact the first part of the ascent is not only through some seriously pretty woods but this is a perfect area for seeing wildcats, pinemartens and red squirrels. Once you are through the gate, the track is back into modern regimented forestry planting in Glen More Forest and is consequently wide and in pretty good condition all the way to the car park. The second half of the route takes you through Rothiemurchus estate and is a most enjoyable mix of track and trail, finishing back on tarmac so that the last uphill is not too arduous. Whereas on many estates in Scotland, bikers are met with annoyance and derision, Rothiemurchus has gone out of its way to provide routes for the biker. This may not have the same appeal as biking into remoter areas but the quality of the tracks and trails along with the superb scenery put it in a class of its own. I have logged only one route but there is a wealth of tracks here (Coylumbridge to Loch Einich is excellent) all of varying standards — so if you want thighs the size of zeppelins or just to spend a couple of days waiting for a pinemarten to show, this is the place for you. Aviemore has all services and as always the Tourist Office will provide information about the best place to stay, eat, hire bikes, etc. (Some bike hire information is available on page 107.)

Route Log

00.00m (00.00km) Car park by Loch Morlich. When setting off, turn right out of it.

00.95 (01.50) Loch Morlich watersports on the right.

01.05 (01.70) Loch Morlich youth hostel and sports holiday centre, shop and cafe.

01.14 (01.85) Telephone.

01.19 (01.90) Information centre and car park.

01.28 (02.06) Turn left, signposted Reindeer Centre.

01.32 (02.12) Fancied yourself as Father Christmas? Now is your chance!

01.91 (03.07) Glen More Lodge Outdoor Centre and Mountain Rescue Post.

02.00 (03.21) End of tarmac, locked bar (easy to get round).

02.28 (03.66) Keep straight.

02.70 (04.34) Keep straight.

03.12 (05.00) An Lochan Uaine on the right.

03.50 (05.63) Y-junction, take the left fork. Leaving Caledonian Pine forest now.

03.58 (05.76) Ford followed by a rubbly hill. This stretch shows signs of being flooded after heavy rains.

03.87 (06.22) Ryvoan Bothy. Open to stay in, one room in very decent condition.

04.62 (07.43) Cattle grid, enter Abernethy Forest Nature Reserve.

05.97 (09.60) Alternative little loop here. Log continues straight but you can go left and past Rynettin Cottage.

06.14 (09.88) Bear left on main track.

07.26 (11.68) Crossroads: if on log route, keep straight; if on alternative track, turn left.

07.33 (11.80) Gate, path round it, turn left onto super smooth track.

08.36 (13.45) Bear right, keeping to main drag.

08.78 (14.12) Bear left.

08.81 (14.17) Tarmac, turn left.

10.00 (16.10) Telephone box.

10.29 (16.55) Turn left, signposted Tulloch Moor.

12.96 (20.85) Main road, bear left.

13.86 (22.30) Turn left after the pine wood; there is a sign on the left fence of the wood to Milton Cottage.

14.37 (23.12) Track forks, keep straight.

15.35 (24.70) Cattle grid, gate (not locked). You are now back in Glen More Forest Park.

15.43 (24.82) Keep straight, track joins.

16.28 (26.20) Fork, keep right. Track going left not marked on 1991 OS map.

17.23 (27.72) Crossroads, keep straight.

18.01 (29.00) Main road, turn right, Loch Morlich car park on your left.

18.18 (29.60) Turn left, main bridge locked, cross via footbridge.

18.40 (29.60) Keep straight.

19.29 (31.03) Turn right, signposted to Piccadilly and Lairig Ghru.

19.35 (31.13) Locked gate, stile to climb over.

20.20 (32.50) Crossroads in a clearing in the wood – keep straight, signed to Aviemore.

20.90 (33.62) Keep straight, do not ford river.

21.06 (33.88) Bear right, do not ford river.

21.09 (33.93) Turn left over bridge.

21.10 (33.94) After the bridge the trail joins track, turn right.

21.19 (34.10) Y-fork, bear left signed to Loch an Eilein.

22.34 (35.95) Ford (small footbridge).

22.60 (36.36) T-Junction. You have reached Loch an Eilein. Turn right. Left is not a right of way for bikers.

22.90 (36.84) The famous castle on the island is visible around here. The building of the castle is not documented but it is known to have existed in 1296. It is the site of many skirmishes, the most notable in 1690 when defeated Jacobites from the Battle of Cromdale beseiged the castle. The defenders were led by Dame Grizel Mor Grant, widow of the fifth laird, who was said to have cast the lead bullets for her men during the attack.

23.02 (37.03) Locked gate.

23.07 (37.11) Cottage.

23.21 (37.34) Keep straight.

23.37 (37.60) End of track. Tarmac, turn right.

23.41 (37.66) Bear right off road. Track restarts.

23.71 (38.14) Fork, keep straight.

23.77 (38.24) High locked gate. There is a little through-way for walkers which it is possible to get a bike through (unless you are laden with panniers).

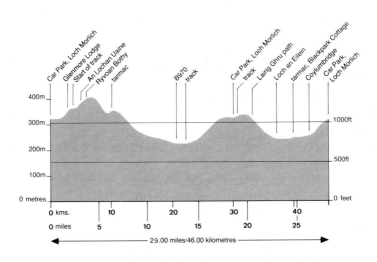

23.94 (38.52) Locked gate – walk-over stile.
24.42 (39.29) Tarmac. Blackpark cottage. Bear left.
25.02 (40.25) Turn right onto main road.
25.75 (41.43) Campsite on the right.
25.80 (41.51) Coylumbridge.
25.85 (41.60) Keep straight, main road B970 turns left to Nethy
  Bridge.
29.00 (46.00) Loch Morlich car park.

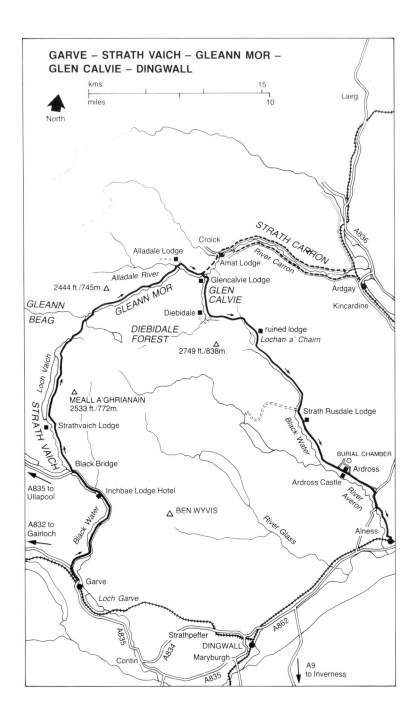

GARVE – STRATH VAICH – GLEANN MOR –
GLEN CALVIE – DINGWALL

kms.   15
miles   10

North

Lairg

STRATH CARRON

Croick
Alladale Lodge
Amat Lodge
River Carron
Alladale River
Glencalvie Lodge
2444 ft./745m. △
GLEANN MOR
GLEN
CALVIE
Ardgay
A836
Kincardine

GLEANN
BEAG

Diebidale
DIEBIDALE
FOREST
ruined lodge
Lochan a' Chairn
2749 ft./838m. △

Loch Vaich

MEALL A'GHRIANAIN
2533 ft./772m. △
Strathvaich Lodge

Strath Rusdale Lodge

Black Water

STRATH VAICH

Black Bridge

A835 to
Ullapool

Inchbae Lodge Hotel

BURIAL CHAMBER
Ardross
Ardross Castle
River
Averon

A832 to
Gairloch

Black Water

BEN WYVIS △

River Glass

Alness

Garve
Loch Garve

A835

A834

Strathpeffer
DINGWALL
Maryburgh

A862

A9
to Inverness

Contin

A835

11

Garve – Strath Vaich – Gleann Mor – Glencalvie – Dingwall

Area information

The most extensive land uses in this area are deer forests, forestry and hydro-electricity. Although the potential for power generation was recognised before the last war, it was not until 1943 that the Hydro-Electric Development (Scotland) Act established the North of Scotland Hydro Board which combined its brief to provide national power supplies with a social commitment to supply domestic electricity to the glens. The second part of the development created reservoirs in Strath Vaich and Loch Glascarnoch. While the hydro development provided a very welcome boost to employment in the area, the flooding of the glens meant the loss of valuable wintering ground for the red deer and required some modifications to farm management of sheep and cattle.

Red deer, the largest surviving land animal left in Britain, are prolific round here. The calves are born in June after a gestation period of eight months. They grow quickly and after about ten days are able to follow their mother wherever she goes. In March the red deer stags lose their antlers, the new ones growing during the summer months. At first the antlers are covered in velvet but by mid-August this has usually been shed and the stag is in 'hard antler'. Hinds and stags live apart for most of the year, only coming together in late September/October for the 'rut'. For the duration of the mating season red deer stags eat very little, spending their time defending their hinds and territories from intruders. At this time of year the hills resound with the sound of stags roaring and you will often see stags fighting each other, a thrilling sight. Since adult red deer have no predators of any worth, deer forests hold an annual cull in order to keep numbers at a level commensurate with the amount of grazing available. Most estates use this cull to weed out old beasts that are unlikely to survive the winter and stags with poor antler conformation, so that only the strongest and the best breed with the hinds. The start of the stalking season is the beginning of July

Early morning by Loch Vaich

but most traditional estates do not commence until August. The season closes on October 20th, after which the cull of old and infertile hinds starts.

Because Easter Ross has numerous wooded and afforested areas, roe deer are also plentiful here. Roe are the 'bambis' of our native deer population. The young, born in late May, are the tiny dappled creatures which melt even the hardest hearts, except those of foresters: roe deer, once inside a young plantation, can create havoc by eating the trees' leaders. Roe deer are much smaller and daintier than red deer and prefer woodland to the wild open hills and rose gardens to woodland. It is said that the best antidote to roe munching away at your prize floribundas is to hang bags of human hair from the bushes. Bald rose-growers should think twice before moving to Easter Ross!

Like red deer, roe bucks will lose and regrow their antlers, but at a different time of year. A mature buck casts his antlers around the end of November and has a set, fully formed and free of velvet, by the end of the following April. You may also see a sika deer on this ride. These are not indigenous to Britain, having been introduced from Japan in 1889 to Achanalt, near Garve. The deer were enclosed until the 1914-18 war when they were released onto the hill. In size a sika deer is bigger than a roe but smaller than a red deer. They are hardy, compact animals and have adapted well to Scotland. Their summer coat is an attractive rich chestnut, profusely dappled with white; their winter coat by contrast is almost black. The rutting cry of the sika is quite different from the roar of a red stag — it is a strange, high-pitched screaming whistle repeated three times. They also have an alarm call which is a single high-pitched whistle. Most estates try to eliminate sika as they tend to breed with red deer and thus endanger the integrity of Scotland's native red deer population.

When I biked this route there was not a sheep to be seen — what irony since it was the advent of sheep that forced the native human population out of the glens in the nineteenth century. In Ross the sheep figures alone tell the story — from a few thousand in 1780 to 252,000 by 1854 and 391,000 by 1869. Once cleared of people, an owner's estate could be leased to lowland stockmasters to graze their cheviot sheep. At the time, it offered a rich prospect: a laird's debts could be paid and his fortune assured by the stroke of a pen, as it were. The Clearances were justified by landowners on the grounds that they were improving the life of the Highlanders by removing them from a life of poverty, ignorance and superstition.

Time to concentrate!

Looking back to Dibbiedale Lodge and Glen Calvie

To a laird who owned a glen which supported, say, five communities of people who, to his mind, gave him little more than their affection and loyalty, the fact that by replacing them with four shepherds, their dogs and three thousand cheviots would make him richer than many Englishmen, was temptation enough. Some lairds protested against the inhumanity involved but greed was more powerful than compassion and for sixty years the Clearances continued with increasing intensity. In 1792 there was a peaceful uprising against the sheep in Easter Ross. It was a local climax of popular feeling which had previously only expressed itself through sporadic attacks on the sheep and abuse of shepherds and their masters. Two hundred people gathered the cheviots and drove them to Strath Rusdale but this act of bravery was suppressed, the sheep rescued and the small rebellion snuffed out. The event passed into legend and for many years served as inspiration to future dissenters. Some of the Clearances were completed quietly and without resistance but there were a few inflamed episodes, one of which, at Glencalvie in 1845, was reported by a journalist with *The Times*. The people in their desperation made a public appeal for asylum and resettlement. But despite the flood of unfavourable publicity, the Clearance was completed. Thereafter the lairds adopted a policy of removing only one or two families a year which meant less likelihood of either resistance or publicity. These were terrible times for the Highlander – two generations had seen the banning of highland dress, the right to speak their own language in the new schools, and widespread eviction from their own homes.

Ardross means the Height or Point of Ross. The area first belonged to the Ross family (a clan that made sure that unless your name was Ross in that northern area, you might as well not have been born) before being taken over by a Mackenzie in the middle of the seventeenth century, after which it was bought by the first Duke of Sutherland. In 1845 the estate was sold again to an Alexander Matheson, sixty thousand acres at a cost of £90,000. Matheson was interested in land drainage and had fixed ideas on the size of farms. He devised a system of 'club' farms with leases of fourteen to nineteen years, each farm with two to fourteen tenants, and was also the first landlord in Ross ever to reduce rents.

The old Ardross Castle was situated north of the church: the present one, nearer the river, was built in 1846 of sandstone which was quarried in the Black Isle, the blocks being brought by sailing ship

In Gaelic, Alness means a marshy place or bog, describing the estuary of the Alness river which in earlier times had several outlets to the sea. With the great industrial expansion of the oil industry at Invergordon and Nigg, Alness has become a dormitory town but despite this it relies on tourism for much of its wealth. This used to be a great idea for illicit whisky-making: now Alness has only one (legal) distillery, the Dalmore, established in 1839.

Strathpeffer is an extraordinary collection of Victorian hotels and villas set on a wooded hillside. The first mention of the springs on the Cromarty estate was in 1772 and by the end of the century the town had become a spa. At first its fortunes fluctuated but great expansion came with the arrival of the railway in 1885. The summer months were the busiest with a special sleeper bringing tourists from London. On arrival they consulted one of the local doctors as to the strength of the spring water and the type of bath likely to be most beneficial. The spa was open from 7.30 am and, to ensure that patrons rose in good time, a piper used to tour the main roads and terraces in full blow from 7 o'clock onwards.

Map: OS Landranger nos. 20, 21 and 26. If you are biking only the section from Garve to Alness, you will not need map 26.

Distance: 49.60 miles, 80.00 kilometres. This distance is from Garve to Alness. Should you miss trains and then their connections, or decide to bike the whole route, then you will need to add another 21 miles (34 kilometres).

Difficulty: easy

Time: Owing to the slightly awkward logistics here, the only guide I can give you is that it took me one long day to bike from Garve to Alness, catch a train to Dingwall and then bike back to Garve. If you are starting at Garve and being met at Alness or Strath Carron, one day is plenty.

Logistics: by train to Garve station, by car on the A832(T) Muir of Ord to Garve road, or the A834 Dingwall road.

Route description
27.60 miles (44.40km) of track, trail and track with tarmac strips, 22.00 miles (35.39km) of tarmac.

Good shelter

If you are only interested in riding track, then the best part of this ride is from Garve to Alness. If, on the other hand, you are interested in biking as a general tourist then the whole tour is for you.

Because the track traverses traditional deer forests, it is important that you telephone the keepers first to make sure of their permission before you set out. They are so friendly and helpful that this is mostly a matter of courtesy − although nonetheless important for that. The time to avoid biking is from the beginning of August to mid-October, the estates' busiest time with the deer stalking season. This is especially so with Glencalvie (which is let during these months) since the route uses their front drive and goes past their front door. Not to be able to bike through here in August and September is hardly an imposition as it is the worst time of year for rain and midges. Telephone numbers of estate keepers:

Strath Vaich − Ian, 089975 226.

Gleann Mhor − Richard Munroe, 08633 338.

Glencalvie − John Gordon, 08633 319.

If you are going to use the railway as part of your journey, don't forget to book your bike onto the train. If you are not sure which train you will catch, it is better to book it onto several rather than be turned away and ruin your ride. I biked this route in a long day but this hardly gave me time either to savour the magnificence of the hills and glens or to lie under an ancient Caledonian pine in the hot sun and enjoy Scotland's most magical asset — peace and quiet.

The track, which is excellent throughout, takes you through the finest deer forests of Easter Ross, each glen a complete contrast to the one before. This is big country indeed, with remnants of ancient Caledonian Forest standing impressively against the heather-clad hills, giving you a glimpse of what this land must have looked like in times past. On the Strath Vaich section I passed a stag, 20 yards off the track, lying neatly curled up in the heather looking out over the loch. Or so I thought. It was in fact dead (of natural causes) and had just stiffened where it was sitting. You could wish for no finer last view.

My apologies to Alness but it is not the most exciting place in Scotland. Dingwall, the ancient capital of Scotland, and Strathpeffer, Victoriana at its best (or worst), are well worth visiting. If you are thinking of taking your time on this tour there are plenty of attractive places to camp in the glens or if you want to stay in Bed and Breakfast, Strathpeffer has a wonderful selection. There are no services once you leave Garve, itself a tiny outpost, so if you need to stock up with food etc. then Dingwall is the best town from a limited selection. If you are a health food and fresh fruit-and-veg fan, then you would be wise to shop in Inverness on your way. Inchbae Hotel (log mile 06.39) is very friendly and has delicious home-made soup, bar meals, etc.

Route Log

00.00m (00.00km) Garve railway station. Turn left out of the station towards the main A835(T).
00.09 (00.14) Straight on through the gate and onto the pavement.
00.26 (00.41) Garve Hotel.
00.86 (01.38) Junction, keep straight, signposted Ullapool A835.
02.20 (03.53) Blackwater river, lay-by with toilets.
06.39 (10.28) Inchbae Hotel.
08.50 (13.67) Turn right before Black Bridge.
10.80 (17.37) Locked gate.
12.81 (20.60) Locked gate, track starts.
13.53 (21.76) Fork, bear left, small dam ahead.

Early morning sun on Deannich Lodge

16.18 (26.03) Derelict house and barn.

18.37 (29.55) Fork, keep straight.

19.95 (32.10) Fork, turn right.

20.29 (32.64) Time to get wet! Fairly deep ford.

20.39 (32.80) Ford.

20.46 (32.92) Deannich Lodge, turn left.

24.76 (39.83) Ruined house, fabulous Caledonian Pines.

26.77 (43.07) T-junction, turn right.

28.42 (45.72) Fork right for Glencalvie Lodge, left for alternative route to Strath Carron.

28.73 (46.22) Glencalvie Lodge. Go through the gates and then keep left with the main lodge on your right. Keep left down a slope, past the keeper's cottage where the track bears right.

31.61 (50.86) Fork, bear left.

33.87 (54.50) Iron gate with spikes, not locked at the time of riding, awkward but not impossible to negotiate if locked.

34.86 (56.08) Ruined lodge, boat house.

36.12 (58.11) Watch out for bridge collapse on the downhill.

36.85 (59.29) Ford, track becomes derelict, tarmac trail.

37.04 (59.59) Barrier of rocks, track returns.

37.21 (60.00) Gate, forestry.
39.27 (63.18) Fork, keep straight.
39.81 (64.05) Fork, keep straight.
40.41 (65.00) Gate and single-track road proper, old mill-race on the right.
42.48 (68.35) Fork, keep straight.
44.60 (71.76) Keep straight, drive to Ardross Castle on the right.
44.70 (71.92) Signpost left to Strathy, keep straight.
45.94 (73.91) Y-fork, unsignposted, keep right.

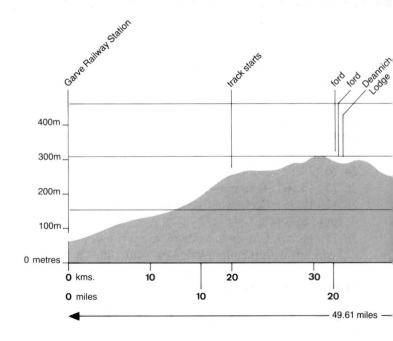

46.41 (74.67) Main A836, turn right.

47.50 (76.42) Turn left, signposted byway to Alness and Invergordon.

49.00 (78.84) Alness.

49.26 (79.25) T-junction, main street, turn left, signposted to the station.

49.52 (79.67) Turn right by the war memorial and then instantly right again.

49.60 (80.00) Alness station.

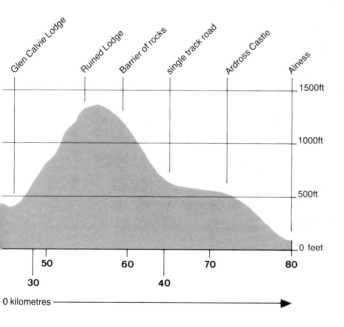

Tourist Information Centres and British Rail/Scotrail

Tourist information centres etc.

Aberfoyle* 08772-352
Aviemore 0479-810363
Ballater* 03397-55306
Balmoral Estate Office 03397-42334
Braemar* 03383-600
Edinburgh 031-557-1700
Fort William and Lochaber 0397-703781
Glasgow 041-227-4878
Glenfinnan Railway Museum 0397-83295
Glenfinnan Information Centre (National Trust) 0397-83250
Glen More Visitor Centre 0479-861220
Inverness 0463-234353
Oban 0631-63122
Pitlochry 0796-2215
Rothiemurchus Visitors' Centre 0479-810858
Strathpeffer* 0997-21415
Strontian* 0967-2131

* denotes offices which are closed in winter (effectively, mid-October to Easter).

British Rail/Scotrail Stations

Edinburgh 031-556-2451
Fort William 0397-703791
Glasgow 041-204-2844

Inverness 0463-238924
Oban 0631-63083

Bike Parts and Suppliers, Bike Hire

This list does not cover all shops in Scotland. It is intended only as a guide to parts stockists, repairers and hire in the general area of the tours. For additional information please contact the Scottish Tourist Board which is very helpful (see previous page). The shops marked with an asterisk (*) hold a good range of Shimano parts but if even these prove unsatisfactory then Madison (Newcastle), telephone 091-261-9995, will post direct to you.

Aberdeen
Cycling World, 460 George Street. 0224-632994*

Aviemore
Ellisbrigham. 0479-810175
Speyside Sports. 0497-810656
Sporthouse. 0479-810655
Sportshire, Nethybridge. 0479-82333
Slochd Ski Sport, Carrbridge. 0479-84666
Inverdruie, Rothiemurchus. 0479-810787

Buckie
Horizon Cycle Hire. 0542-33070

Dufftown
I. & H. Massie, 5 Fife Street. 0340-20559/20906

Dundee
Nicholson, 2 Forfar Road. 0382-461212*

Edinburgh
Edinburgh Bicycle Co-Op, 8 Alvanley Terrace, Whitehouse Lane. 031-228-1368*
Robin Williamson, 26 Hamilton Place, Stockbridge. 031-225-3286*

Fort William
Off-Beat Bikes (Dave Austen). 0397-702663
Lees Cycle Hire. 0397-704204

Glasgow
Dales, 150 Dobbies Loan. 041-332-2705*

Glencoe
Glencoe Bike Hire (Steve or Nancy Kennedy). 08552-685

Glenfinnan
Clark, Craiglea, Lochailort. 06877-273

Inverness
Thorntons, 23 Castle Street. Shop: 0463-222810; Workshop: 0463-235078*
Highland Cycles, 26 Greig Street. 0463-710462*

Kinlochleven
Leven Cycles. 21-22 Leven Road. 08554-614*

Oban
The Cycle Shop, Tregard Road (Hire & Repair). 0631-66996

Tomintoul
Bridge of Brown Tea Room. 08074-335

Restaurants

Finding good home cooking at a reasonable price can be difficult in Scotland. When in doubt, it is usually more rewarding to go vegetarian. The following suggestions either always have a selection of vegetarian meals or will cook to order.

Name	Town	Tel. No.
Osprey Hotel	Kingussie	0540-661510
Culloden Pottery	Inverness	0667-462749
Culloden House	Inverness	0463-790461
Brookes Wine Bar	Inverness	0463-225662
Braeval Old Mill	Aberfoyle	08772-711
Cuilfail Hotel	Kilmelford	08522-274
The Lorne Pub	Oban	0631-66766
The Oban Inn	Oban	0631-62484
Littlejohns	Perth	0738-39888
	Stirling	0786-63222
Cruachan House, Dinner and/or B&B	Dalmally near Oban	08382-496
Inchbae Lodge Hotel	Garve	09975-269

Bothy Accommodation

Bothy	OS Map no.	Map Ref.	Estate
Ryvoan	36	005115	Glenmore — open to anyone
Tearnait	49	742472	Ardtornish — open to M.B.A.

Glossary of Scottish Words used in this book

Beallach: a small saddle between two higher parts of a hill.
Bothy: a single-storied building traditionally used to house unmarried seasonal labourers.
Brae: a steep slope.
Burn: a stream.
Cairn: a man-made pile of stones, usually conical; also a fox's den in a very stoney place.
Croft: a smallholding.
Dour: sullen, grim: how a shepherd will look after you have scattered his flock or left the gate open.
Drover: one who drove livestock to market, often over very long distances.
Factor: the agent of a landlord.
Fank: a pen, or system of pens, used for handling sheep.
Forest (as in deer forest): an estate used for deer stalking. Often the only trees found nowadays in these forests are modern plantations.
Guid tackle: good food.
Kirk: church.
Laird: landed proprietor; sometimes used sarcastically, in the same way as *sahib.*
Lodge: where the laird of a forest occasionally resides.
Marching (with): of estates, sharing a common boundary.
Munro: a hill over 3,000ft (915m) in height.
Outwith: outside, not near, more distant (also in relation to time).
Policy: usually in the plural, the pleasure grounds of a mansion.
Pursy: of people, short-breathed and fat; of horses broken-winded.
Shieling: a shepherd's summer hut, summer grazing.
Spate: a flood in a burn or river.
Steadings: farm building.
Strath: a valley of considerable extent, larger than a glen and usually fertile.

NOTES